Beyond The Imprint

A New Modality

For Mental Health Practitioners

And Those Seeking Their Help

Kate O'Connell, LPC

ISBN-13: 978-1540757753

www.oconnellkate.com

With love and gratitude, this book is dedicated to my parents and siblings who deeply imprinted me, and to all of my clients and teachers who influenced my thinking, developed my skill-set and informed all of the themes embodied within this modality.

Contents

Adolescence

Adulthood

Beyond the Imprint (BTI)

BTI Therapy

Author's Imprint

Preface

In 1986 at the age of twenty-five, I began to explore holistic and alternative methods of healing which subsequently led to my studying and training with a number of different teachers and healers operating from within a variety of different spiritual and metaphysical frameworks.

In 1997, I co-founded a spiritual retreat center in the Adirondacks with a Cherokee medicine woman and shaman where clients came from across the country to experience the sacred healing ceremonies of Sweat Lodge, Vision Quest and Soul Retrieval. During this time I developed the ability to assess and work with people on an energetic level.

However, I also recognized that only a very small percentage of the population chose to access alternative healing modalities such as these because of cultural conditioning within Western medicine and its singular focus on the scientific model of evidence-based practices. I began to understand that in order to be truly effective as a 'healing agent' practicing within the western world; it was important for me to become proficient in western models of assessment and care.

So in 2003, I decided to come down from the mountain and pursue a graduate degree in *Mental Health Counseling* within the field of *Psychology*. After graduating, I spent the next several years working for agencies that provided mental health services for at-risk, under-served populations. During this time I developed the ability to assess and assist children, adolescents, couples and families achieve increased stability and equilibrium in their lives while advocating for them within the legal, social and academic systems.

I am currently in private practice in Charlottesville, Virginia as a *Child and Family Therapist* in which all of what I've learned while 'on the mountain', in the classroom and working within the various systems, influences my work with clients whose ages span the entire developmental spectrum, addressing a wide variety of issues.

My clinical and metaphysical experiences have shaped the kind of therapist I have become, including what my beliefs are regarding the efficacy of different therapeutic models of intervention, the rationale behind them and the expectations placed on individuals and families whose circumstances have forced them to interact with the systems that have been established to protect them from themselves, each other and the larger collective.

Most importantly, my experience as a mental health clinician over the past several years continues to reveal inherent pathologies within the very systems that have been put in place to intervene on behalf of individuals and their family members who are struggling to achieve mental and emotional stability. In other words, I can't help but notice how consistently the inherent pathologies of the agencies reflect the pathologies of the clients they serve.

This observation has led me to focus more intently on the quality of the therapeutic relationship since the agencies I'm referring to are comprised of therapists, counselors and social workers. It seems logical to consider that if the larger organism is ill; then we would want to direct our attention to the cells that make up that organism.

This book is an attempt to focus such attention and identify how critical it is for mental health practitioners to be involved at all times in an ongoing, exhaustive, self-assessment regarding unconscious perceptions, beliefs, behavioral and relationship patterns. To not be so involved, severely limits the practitioner's ability to facilitate a healing experience for the client. My participation on both sides of the client/practitioner model over the years has allowed an ongoing inquiry on this subject and the subsequent insights I have acquired have become the primary motivation for creating the modality described in this book.

In addition, the content enclosed is intended to be a comprehensive overview of what I consider to be the most important areas of focus when working with individuals and families whose identified goal is to achieve increased health and well-being with the self and the relationships they have formed with others.

In short, I have written the book that I would have wanted to read while still in graduate school; thereby closing the significant gap between the theories that are taught and the reality of what is actually occurring in mental health agencies and therapist's offices across this country. It's an attempt to develop further clarity for myself as both client and practitioner. Hopefully it will assist others in their attempts to facilitate healing as well as those seeking it.

Introduction

When I was two, I spoke my first word and that word was, *"Alleluia"*.

Now, I assume that when other prophets throughout history have made similar utterances, they were recognized by large, devotional audiences for being in possession of magical powers and speaking from divine inspiration. In my case, however, when I spoke my first word and my first word was divinely inspired; I spoke it to an 'Audience of One'. And that audience was my mother. And no one believed her.

The Uncarved Block

The basic Taoist principle of the *Uncarved Block* embodies the understanding that people and things in their original simplicity contain their own natural power; power that becomes diminished when that simplicity is changed; power that becomes diminished when the block is carved by some outside force.

In my case, I have come to understand that one of the first significant carvings which began to change my shape was in response to the first word I spoke. And because my first word was not 'bike' or 'car' or 'ball', my shape took on the carving:

"That can't be true because she's not that special."

It's entirely possible that this initial carving was predestined and consistent with karmic imprinting when you consider that the family of origin through which I incarnated in this lifetime was not a family of Taoists living in a remote region of China, but rather, Irish Catholics living in the suburbs of Toronto.

Beyond the Imprint (BTI) is my attempt at creating a modality for mental health practitioners and those seeking their help to identify and address what it is that informs all of our beliefs, perceptions and subsequent behaviors which we unconsciously rely on every day in an attempt to get our emotional and physical needs met.

I believe that our dysfunctional relationship patterns with self and others stem from our imprinting at the molecular level that each and every one of us carries in our physical bodies as cellular memory. This memory has been recorded through the respective DNA of our maternal and paternal lineages that we've inherited as well as from everything we've ever experienced in our environments beginning at the moment of conception.

Because minds 'think' and bodies 'feel', I refer to the mind as a CPU processor with a finite cache of memory that creates the stories we form around these experiences. Rarely, if ever, are these stories accurate. Instead, they end up being our greatest defense mechanism by ensuring that we never truly connect to the feelings we carry at the molecular level as memory in response to our experiences.

So if we go to our therapist and engage in talk therapy sessions every week in which we tell the same stories over and over; those cellular imprints will actually end up being reinforced, usually within the framework of a victim/perpetrator dynamic. We *think* we feel better because we just vented all of our frustrations regarding someone or something that we believe is responsible for us not getting our needs met. However, in this scenario, no lasting changes will occur because nothing internal has shifted. As long as our focus is primarily directed outside of us in order to identify what needs to change, nothing will.

Even if we leave our current personal or professional relationship with the hope and expectation of having a different experience with the next one; we won't. The names and locations might change, but the patterns will always persist.

Since these patterns are specific to, and reflections of, our own wound imprinting at the cellular level; the primary focus within the therapeutic venue should always be directed towards the self.

Healing requires that we overcome whatever obstacles have prevented us from achieving mental, emotional and physical balance. Understanding all of the ways in which we've been diminished by outside forces that left an indelible mark or 'carving' on us at the cellular level is the key to dissolving those imprints so that we may reclaim our original simplicity and natural power.

Beyond the Imprint (BTI) is my attempt to help all of us, clients and practitioners alike, move beyond the confines of our respective cellular imprinting towards greater self-actualization so that we may experience the joy, peace, love and freedom made manifest on such a profound and radical journey.

"I throw roses into the abyss and say:

Here is my thanks to the monster

who did not devour me."

-Friedrich Nietzsche -

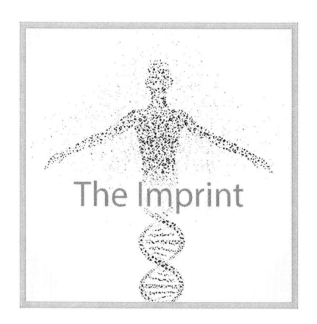

The Imprint

THE IMPRINT

❖ *All of our thoughts, beliefs, perceptions, behaviors and relationship patterns have been shaped and determined by our respective DNA lineages and all of our experiences beginning at conception in the form of cellular memory referred to as 'imprinting'.*

❖ *Prenatal, perinatal and childhood experiences which should include appropriate environmental stimulus and responsiveness to our needs not only prevents distress, but also ensures that the limbic brain which receives and processes sensations, feelings and emotions 'imprints' these experiences as cellular memory in the body, validating our right to exist.*

❖ *If these experiences are less nurturing and more painful, our limbic system begins to 'imprint' these experiences on the cellular level as distorted expressions of love.*

❖ *This sets us up to recreate these experiences in a cyclical fashion throughout life, informing chronic dysfunctional relationship patterns in an unconscious attempt to get our physical and emotional needs met.*

❖ *Our DNA may be the blueprint of life, but it turns out that our environment is what influences our genetic functioning, including our thoughts, feelings and beliefs in response to our experiences.*

❖ *How we develop in utero in response to our mother's stress levels, the degree of trauma we experience at birth, how securely we are able to attach to our primary caregivers and how nurturing our childhood environments are, appear to be the most important factors influencing development and future generations.*

The Science of Epigenetics

I became aware of the science *of Epigenetics* a number of years ago through the work of Bruce Lipton after reading his book *"The Biology of Belief"*. It was groundbreaking in so far as he combined quantum physics and cell biology to identify the mechanisms in which cells receive and process information. Although the science of *Epigenetics* had begun to emerge in the early 1970's, Dr. Lipton's thesis presented a concise and comprehensive overview of these discoveries in a manner and language that lay people such as myself could understand and apply to their lives in a meaningful way.

Further research in this field continues to expand on our understanding of how our DNA and subsequent perceptions, beliefs, behaviors, relationship patterns and experiences are being influenced by our environment and the individuals who inhabit it.

These concepts are a major thread in the fabric which I am weaving together as a framework to guide my clients on their journey to greater health and well-being. Because I am not well-versed in this particular branch of science; I cannot describe it using terms such as *methyl groups, histone spools, glucocorticoid receptors* and *acetyl groups,* but somehow I am able to grasp the implications of what this research has to offer. As a result, a large part of my work focuses on what the implications for our respective futures are once we have that understanding.

During the first few sessions of meeting with someone I will begin to differentiate between the 'mind' and the 'body'. One of the ways I do this is to start with the most important distinction and that is that minds 'think' and bodies 'feel'. The mind is similar to a CPU processor; which holds a very limited, finite cache of memory. Its primary function is to process the signals that the physical body is constantly sending to it as well as create a myriad of stories around what it is we think we are experiencing in response to those signals. The bulk of our memories are really encoded in the fifty trillion cells of our body. Everything that we've ever experienced is recorded in these cells. Now add to that the understanding that we are also carrying within our DNA all of the memories from our respective maternal and paternal lineages, their respective lineages and so on and so on and we now begin to have a much fuller understanding of the scope of what is influencing our experiences, including why we continue to cycle through the same patterns regardless of how undesirable or painful they may be.

Simply put, all of our thoughts, beliefs, perceptions, behaviors and relationship patterns are being determined by our DNA lineages, our experiences beginning at the perinatal stage and continuing throughout childhood, adolescence and adulthood. What was modeled for us and projected onto us that we accepted as being true about ourselves, including our environment and those we were in relationship with, also shaped our perceptions and subsequent beliefs. The key to climbing out from underneath all of this is to begin to become aware of this unconscious imprinting that has shaped and determined our limiting perceptions and beliefs. Once we become aware, we can begin to participate more consciously in our experiences and learn how to change our response to whatever is happening. In doing so, we ultimately change our experience.

A great way to begin is by becoming more body-focused since this is where all of our memory is held. I ask my clients to begin cultivating awareness around the moment in which they become 'triggered'. It will always be in response to something or someone who is doing something that has resulted in our nervous systems becoming dysregulated. We can notice this when our adrenals become activated. If we don't recognize it when this happens then we have another opportunity to do so when our defense mechanisms show up in response to our adrenals becoming activated. It is precisely at this moment that we want to hit the 'pause' button and create a space in time between the stimulus and our response to the stimulus long enough to make a conscious choice to *not* defend ourselves.

Eventually what we come to realize is that whatever 'triggered' us was a stimulus in the environment that touched on a memory that we were holding onto to in one of the fifty trillion cells in our body and it just so happened that the stimulus resonated with the memory. Once 'triggered', the memory then sends out signals to the brain and body indicating that we are not safe. In response to those signals, the adrenals become activated which then sets into motion a myriad of chemical and hormonal responses within the brain and body that positions us into a 'fight or flight' response. It is at this time that we begin to react through some defensive posturing. Depending on the stimulus and the energetic 'charge' around the memory, our defensive posturing and subsequent expression could cover a wide range of responses. That is why it is so helpful to begin to practice hitting the 'pause' button because, in all likelihood, the reactivity that we bring to the current situation is usually, if not always, way out of proportion to what is actually occurring in the moment. A really good example of this would be what unfolds during 'road rage'. From my perspective, whether I'm observing it or participating in it; the response is never about what is actually happening, but rather an over-reaction to an unconscious memory of another time from our past in which our physical and emotional safety was threatened.

Beginning to work consciously with the understanding of *Epigenetics* and cellular memory helps move us beyond the unending cycles of violence and victimology. We can begin to take a closer look at our defense mechanisms and behavioral patterns and tease apart exactly what it is that we are holding onto that is no longer relevant or appropriate to hold onto given the identification that we are choosing to have a different experience. The *genome* has long been known as the blueprint of life, but the *epigenome* can be thought of as an *Etch a Sketch* in which it is possible to wipe away the memory.

Epigenetics is the science that identifies that our genes are constantly being modified in response to our life experiences and emphasizes that our perceptions of what it is we're experiencing is what shapes our biology and ultimately determines what we experience. What I find most exciting about this premise is that it allows all of us to move beyond our victimology regardless of how horrific or traumatic our past may have been in order to create a much more empowering future; one full of infinite possibilities imbued with love, happiness and peace. In doing so, we honor our ancestors and future generations to come who will no longer have to inherit the stress and trauma of prior generations.

Summary

❖ *Our DNA and subsequent perceptions, beliefs, behaviors and relationship patterns are being determined and influenced by our environment and the individuals who inhabit it.*

❖ *Our memories are encoded in the fifty trillion cells of our body, including everything that we've ever experienced and all of the memories from our respective maternal and paternal lineages.*

❖ *It is important to become aware of our unconscious imprinting that has shaped and determined our perceptions of self and others so that we may participate more consciously in our experience.*

❖ *By changing our response to what is happening outside of us; we ultimately change our experience which, in turn, changes our biology and behavioral patterns; moving us beyond the unending cycles of violence and victimology.*

Trauma

Prior to becoming a therapist, I believed as the majority of people still do, that trauma and subsequent PTSD are experienced by only a small portion of the population and limited primarily to combat soldiers and first responders such as firefighters, police and EMT's; as well as residents of war-torn countries and victims of catastrophic events. Having now worked in the field of mental health counseling for eleven years in which the first five were spent facilitating intensive in-home services for children and families considered 'at-risk'; I now understand that trauma affects everyone, including myself.

So let's find out how and why this is possible and because this is a very BIG subject; I am offering, for your consideration, a homeopathic overview; one that has been distilled down to its very essence in order to provide a concise understanding within a very limited forum.

Experts within the field of trauma have identified that there are essentially two ways in which an individual can experience trauma. Shock trauma occurs in response to a specific event such an accident, catastrophic event, serious illness, surgery or the sudden and unexpected loss of a loved one. Developmental trauma, on the other hand, is experienced through chronic emotional, psychological, physical or sexual abuse and/or extreme poverty throughout childhood; spanning critical stages of development. As of 1997, statistics indicated that 1 in 3 women and 1 in 5 men in the U.S. had been sexually abused before the age of eighteen and that between 75 and 100 million Americans had experienced childhood sexual and/or physical abuse.

Trauma changes you forever and results in a wide variety of symptoms including, but not limited to; flashbacks, inability to focus, panic attacks, insomnia, depression, anxiety, short attention spans, destructive behaviors and rage. Most, if not all, expressions of mental illness and emotional instability have trauma as an antecedent.

In order to understand trauma we must briefly visit the human brain which is often referred to as the 'trine brain' because it is made up of three parts; the reptilian brain (*instinctual*), the mammalian or limbic brain (*emotional*) and the human or neo-cortex brain (*rational*). When an individual is faced with an overwhelming or life-threatening event; the reptilian/instinctual brain along with our nervous system becomes highly activated or 'charged' in response to the threat. This response is involuntary and instinctual, causing the body to 'freeze' in response to the threat. This immobilization causes the mind to go into an altered state ensuring that no pain is experienced.

Trauma is physiological and will often involve a wide variety of responses including, but not limited to; immobility, panic, inability to breathe or speak and numbness in the body. These responses are a result of the 'energetic charge' and activation of the nervous system being compressed within the experience of immobilization. These mechanics protect us from feeling and often remembering the event. Due to the mind-altering component, trauma ends up being a multidimensional, physiological experience that is almost always difficult to articulate even when it is remembered.

This 'energetic charge' which was mobilized to negotiate the threat must be discharged or it becomes a cellular imprint encoded in the physical body as a memory which could eventually inform a whole host of physical and emotional expressions of disease. Physical movement at the time of the event is critical in being able to discharge the compressed or 'flash-frozen' energy so as not to experience any adverse symptoms as a result of staying immobilized.

Unresolved trauma can lead to a lifetime of victimology and dysfunctional behavioral/relationship patterns. The individual becomes guarded, employing a multitude of defense mechanisms to ensure that they don't feel the pain that would be associated with the original trauma(s). In addition, there is an unconscious attempt to revisit the original trauma(s) in order to resolve what had become deeply encoded in the physical body. This often results in the individual cycling through patterns of trauma throughout their entire lifetime such as accidents and injuries, all of which typically occur within the context of high drama. Adrenals which were activated as part of the nervous system becoming 'charged' at the time of the original trauma(s) end up being chronically activated as part of this cyclical phenomenon. After a while, the experience becomes normalized as a way of being and we now have an entire population suffering from adrenal fatigue as a result of being addicted to the cyclical pattern which results in a myriad of chemicals and hormones being secreted throughout the brain and the body. Most, if not all, of my clients who come to see me are initially encouraged to start taking liquid adrenal support as part of their recovery process.

Because trauma is physiological, the healing of trauma is a process that can only be accessed by developing more conscious, 'body-centered', awareness. There is no need to participate in years of therapy or dredge up deeply suppressed memories. Creating an identity as 'victim' or 'survivor' around the abuse/trauma through membership in support groups or as a perpetual therapy client interferes with one's ability to recover because reliving the emotional pain by telling your story over and over again is re-traumatizing and serves no purpose other than to reinforce the original trauma imprinting. Pharmaceuticals further compound the problem by suppressing feelings and sensations while interfering with the body's innate wisdom to heal. Because our cultural conditioning devalues emotional vulnerability and places an emphasis on the importance of the mind and our ability to endure difficult experiences; we, as a collective, have become extremely disconnected from our physical and instinctual selves. In order to heal from trauma we must reconnect to this aspect of ourselves.

Healing trauma is about restoring wholeness to an organism that has been fragmented or shattered by integrating the aspects of the self that have been 'flash-frozen' in time and space through fear. Somatic-centered modalities have proven to be the most effective treatments to release trauma from the physical body. *Fluid-Dynamic Cranial Sacral Therapy, EMDR, Somatic Emotional Release Therapy* (SERT), *Rolfing, Acupuncture, Reiki, Massage, Tai Chi, Qi Gong* and *Floating* (Sensory Deprivation Tanks) are all modalities that I have experienced and continue to use in my ongoing recovery from trauma and my journey towards increased integration and wholeness.

Trauma imprinting limits our ability to fully engage in life and changes us forever in ways we can never fully comprehend. It interferes with our ability to be intimate with our self and others because from the moment we are traumatized we carry the deep instinctual imprint that we are not safe. Everything we do and all of our beliefs are determined by the fear that is 'flash-frozen' and encoded in the trillions of cells of our body. Well-honed, sophisticated, defense mechanisms, including alcohol, recreational drugs and pharmaceuticals, ensure that we will never fully feel the sensations that come from being in a physical body.

We go through life guarded and distrustful of our environment and the people who inhabit it, including the individuals we are in closest relationship with. We carry shame, guilt and regrets buried deeply within our psyches; believing that we are unworthy of love and acceptance. Recovering from trauma through a gentle, heart-centered, body-focused awareness and approach can be extremely transformative; making it one of the most significant experiences one could ever have in achieving a physical, emotional, psychological and spiritual awakening.

Summary

❖ Trauma is physiological and involves a wide variety of responses including, but not limited to, immobility, panic, inability to breathe or speak and numbness in the body.

❖ These responses are a result of the 'energetic charge' and activation of the nervous system being compressed and immobilized. These mechanisms protect us from feeling and often remembering the event.

❖ This 'energetic charge' which was mobilized to negotiate the threat must be discharged or it becomes a cellular imprint encoded in the physical body as a memory which will eventually create a whole host of physical and emotional expressions of disease.

❖ Unresolved trauma can lead to a lifetime of victimology and dysfunctional relationship patterns. Most, if not all, expressions of mental illness and emotional instability have trauma as an antecedent.

❖ *Trauma imprinting limits our ability to fully engage in life. It changes us forever in ways we can never fully comprehend. It interferes with our ability to be intimate with our self and others because from the moment we are traumatized we carry the deep instinctual imprint that we are not safe.*

❖ *Because trauma is physiological, somatic-centered modalities have proven to be the most effective treatments we have to release trauma from the physical body.*

Conception

CONCEPTION

❖ *Imprinting begins at the moment of conception through the collective DNA of our respective lineages and their accumulative cellular memories, including trauma. This explains inter-generational patterns and expressions of behavior.*

❖ *At the moment of conception, we are implanted in our very first environment; making us vulnerable to imprinting by whatever stressors our mother is being exposed to and her response to those stressors.*

❖ *As a result, our sense of safety and security begins to be encoded as cellular memory before we are even born.*

Pre and Perinatal Psychology

PPNP is a branch of psychology that explores the psychological and physiological implications of prenatal and perinatal experiences of the fetus and developing child. Subjects such as the health and well-being of the mother throughout her pregnancy, the importance of minimizing birth trauma and secure attachment between the child and caregiver, are central themes within *PPNP*. There is growing research which continues to identify that these earliest experiences impact the developing child's overall health and well-being and that these early imprints continue to influence subconscious programming well into adulthood, including the ability to learn and form healthy relationships.

This field began to emerge in the early 1900's when Sigmund Freud's student, Otto Rank, began to develop the theory that birth trauma was a factor in determining one's behaviors later in life. His theory was not embraced by the rest of the medical community, including Freud, and the relationship between student and mentor soured. It was not until the 1960's and '70's, through the work of psychologists John Bowlby and his student, Mary Ainsworth, were the importance of secure attachments, and the various styles of attachment, identified. This resulted in the scientific community being able to accept that early experiences in the womb, during birth and the first few years of life had significant implications for the individual's health and well-being throughout their lifetime.

The science of *Epigenetics,* in combination with *Attachment Theory*, is a large part of the research and understanding that makes up this particular branch of psychology. One of the ongoing arguments between psychologists since the birth of psychology has been the *"Nature vs. Nurture"* debate. This has been ongoing in an attempt to identify whether heredity or environmental factors are primarily responsible for determining the development of an individual; including behavior, intelligence and personality.

In 2001, the first draft of the *Human Genome Project* was published in the journal *"Nature"*. The most startling finding was that the number of human genes was 30 percent fewer than previous estimates. When the project started in 1987, it was estimated that there were as many as a 100,000 genes. It was also assumed that human complexity originated from this number; the greater number of genes; the greater the complexity. So you can only imagine the confusion when only 31,000 protein-encoded genes were discovered. No longer can the argument be made that genetics has the greatest influence on our development. As stated in the previous chapter, our

DNA may be the blueprint of life, but it turns out that the environment is what informs our genetic functioning, including our thoughts and feelings in response to our experiences. How a baby develops in utero in response to mom's stress levels, the degree of trauma experienced at birth, and how securely the child is able to attach to his or her primary caregivers; appears to be the most important factors influencing development and future generations.

Summary

❖ *Early experiences in the womb, during birth and the first few years of life, have significant implications for the individual's health and well-being throughout life, including their ability to learn and form healthy relationships.*

❖ *How a baby develops in utero in response to the mother's stress levels, the degree of trauma experienced at birth, and how securely the child is able to attach to his or her primary caregiver;, appears to be the most important factors influencing development and future generations.*

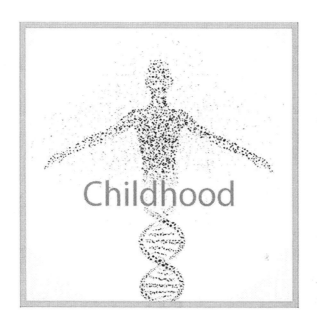

Childhood

CHILDHOOD

❖ Imprinting continues throughout childhood during one of the most vulnerable and critical stages of development.

❖ What is projected onto us and modeled for us by our primary caregivers is being influenced by their own respective and unresolved imprinting, which has been reinforced by centuries of social and cultural conditioning.

❖ Our schemas develop around this conditioning, which informs all of our beliefs and perceptions about our self, others and our environment; including the unconscious need to control or be controlled in order to feel safe and secure.

❖ The fact that we are the only organisms on the planet that are aware that our time in this physical body is finite is what makes us receptive and vulnerable to this conditioning.

❖ *We unconsciously participate in the belief that we must conform to this conditioning in order to ensure our survival.*

Pre and Perinatal Psychology

(*Continued*)

Early childhood is the most critical stage of development given that the brain, in its earliest stages of development, is still organizing. Perinatal experiences which include breastfeeding, constant touch, soothing voices, gentle environmental stimulus and responsiveness to needs not only prevents distress, but also ensures that the limbic brain which receives and processes sensations, feelings and emotions is imprinted in such a way that validates our right to exist. If, on the other hand, our early childhood experiences beginning with gestation are less nurturing and more painful, our limbic system begins to imprint these experiences as representative of love. This, in turn, sets us up to recreate these experiences throughout life informing dysfunctional styles of relationship patterns in an attempt to get our physical and emotional needs met.

Research within the field of *PPNP* has shown that physical, disease expressions and behavioral issues later in life can be traced back to trauma; spanning gestation, birth and early childhood. The baby's nervous system will become 'hard-wired' and create a 'comfort zone' around whatever the initial environment offered in the form of stimulus. If it was primarily painful and frightening; then baby becomes imprinted in both the brain and body to expect this. Consistent with trauma research, he/she will spend the rest of his/her life recreating and attracting into their life these kinds of experiences; ones that are unloving, unkind, stressful, anxiety-provoking and abusive.

Early childhood trauma, combined with our collective conditioning, has created within us an orientation in which we are constantly looking outside of ourselves in an attempt to get our physical and emotional needs met. I believe that when we have an over-reliance on the other to make us feel better about ourselves; we are attempting to compensate for a time in our life in which our basic needs were not met. Our early formative years are the time in which what we take in as loving and nurturing sets us up emotionally and physically for the rest of our lives. If our brains and bodies were not encoded with the fundamental message that we had the right to exist because our caregivers were unresponsive to our needs; then we will be unconsciously seeking this out within all of our relationships throughout our lifetime.

The good news is; now that we are aware of the impact that these early childhood experiences may have had on us; we have the ability to change our current experience. No longer do we have to be victimized by what affected us long before we have any memory of even being alive. Having the understanding that our undesirable experiences are largely influenced by these imprints is the first step in dissolving them. Body work such as *Somatic Emotional Release Therapy* and various modalities within the realm of *Energy Medicine* such as *Cranial Sacral Therapy* are extremely effective in assisting one's healing process at the deepest levels of trauma imprinting.

Summary

❖ Early childhood is the most critical stage of development given that the brain, in its earliest stages of development, is still organizing.

❖ Gentle, soothing and loving perinatal experiences ensures that the limbic brain is imprinted in such a way that validates our right to exist.

❖ Physical, disease expressions and behavioral issues later in life can be traced back to trauma; spanning gestation, birth and early childhood.

❖ The baby's nervous system will become 'hard-wired' and create a 'comfort zone' around whatever the initial environment offered in the form of stimulus. If it was primarily painful and frightening; then the baby becomes imprinted in the brain and the body to expect this.

❖ If we are not encoded with the fundamental messages that we had the right to exist because our caregivers were unresponsive to our needs; we will spend the rest of our lives attracting these kinds of relationships and experiences.

Attachment

Attachment is the emotional bond that develops between a child and a primary caregiver and is considered to be the most important aspect of child development beginning at the moment of birth and continuing throughout childhood.

Early research theorized that attachment or bonding was largely determined by the biological needs of the infant and the caregiver's ability to provide food and meet other physiological needs. However, psychologist Harry Harlow, in the 1950's, conducted a famous experiment in which infant monkeys were given a choice between cuddling with a wire monkey who provided food or with a soft, warm, cloth monkey who did not have food. The overwhelming preference was to hang out with the cloth monkey who provided comfort.

Another psychologist, John Bowlby, held the view that attachment was primarily the infant/child's need for safety and security and was genetically influenced through the motivation to avoid predators. This took the theory to the epigenetic level in which the reciprocal relationship between the genes and the environment were at play. He also identified that secure attachment to a primary caregiver was critical in allowing the developing child to successfully explore their world.

In the 1960's and 70's, Bowlby's student, Mary Ainsworth, built on his theory through her own research by developing a technique to measure attachment. She created the *Ainsworth Strange Situation* which consisted of eight staged episodes involving a mother, a child and a stranger. The various scenarios are as follows:

1. *the mother and child enter a room*
2. *the mother sits down to let the child explore*
3. *an adult stranger enters the room and speaks to the mother and then the child*
4. *the mother then leaves the room and the child is left with the stranger*
5. *the mother then returns and greets the stranger and then comforts the child and the stranger leaves*
6. *the mother then leaves the room again and the child is alone*
7. *the stranger returns*
8. *the mother returns and the stranger leaves*

What was discovered was that the child's reactions to the various scenarios were quite different depending on the pattern of attachment the child had to the mother. Ainsworth identified three different patterns: the *secure attached pattern*, the *avoidant attached pattern* and the *ambivalent attached pattern*. Later, her work was expanded on by a colleague to include a fourth pattern, the *disorganized-disoriented attached pattern.*

The *secure attached pattern* was present when the child used the mother as a home base, seemed at ease in the *Strange Situation* as long as the mother was present; explored independently; may or may not have been upset when she left and immediately went to her when she returned. Children who demonstrated the *avoidant attached pattern* did not seek out close proximity to the mother; did not seem distressed when she left and avoided her when she returned. With the *ambivalent attached pattern*, children displayed positive and negative reactions to the mother and were usually in such close proximity to her that they didn't explore their environment; became anxious before she left; were distressed when she did leave and were ambivalent when she returned, seeking to be close but also hitting and kicking her in anger. The *disorganized-disoriented attached pattern* is the least securely attached pattern. These children demonstrate inconsistent and contradictory behavior by approaching the mother and avoiding contact with her. This pattern suggests tremendous confusion on the child's part.

So how has *Attachment Theory* influenced our understanding of human development during the past forty-five years?

Academically speaking, there are many thoughts in response to this question. A significant amount of research has accumulated in an attempt to tease apart the various styles of attachment that form in response to the various styles of parenting that are practiced. The goal being that the more we understand about this subject; the better we can educate prospective parents on the do's and don'ts of parenting in order to ensure a more securely attached child.

Since attachment is understood to be the basic human need for a child to have a safe and close relationship with a parent or primary caregiver and we know that secure attachment patterns are established when the parent(s) are responsive to the child's needs; securely attached children end up being curious, independent, ego-resilient and successful in forming healthy relationship patterns which then persist into adulthood. This is possible because the parents have provided a safe 'home base' from which the child is able to leave and explore their environment within a range that is developmentally appropriate. As long as the child has a safe place to come back to, they will feel more confident in their ability to explore their external world and more trusting of the people they meet along the way.

Attachment Theory models continue to identify that 80% of children in the United States are securely attached and yet it is also widely accepted that 90% of adult relationships in the United States are co-dependent. From my perspective the latter is more consistent with what I have experienced and observed in both my personal and professional life and would indicate to me that children who grow up to form adult co-dependent relationships could not have possibly met the criteria for being securely attached to their caregiver(s) as children.

In addition, current statistics indicate that one in four children in this country between the ages of 13 and 18 have now been identified as suffering from an anxiety disorder. In 1985, half a million children in the United States met the diagnostic criteria for ADHD and today it is estimated that 5 to 7 million children in this country now have this diagnosis. Three and a half million children have met the criteria for a diagnosis of depression and a recent study showed a 600 percent increase in the diagnosis of pediatric bipolar disorder in children under the age of 13 in the last 10 years. Most of these children are receiving pharmacological interventions despite the absence of longitudinal studies ensuring the safety of such interventions on developing brains that have *not* been funded by pharmaceutical companies. This increasing need to chemically restrain our youth is a growing trend which is alarming many experts in the field of trauma and child development, including myself, and can, at best, be categorized as a massive social experiment.

It is also a great example of how, far too often, the interventions which are widely endorsed by the institutions within our society are completely incongruent with what we've discovered through research and proven to be true regarding human development. As a collective, we have become extremely fearful and distrustful. The perception is that it is far too dangerous to let our children wander beyond our range of vision despite the fact that they are at a much lower risk of being victims of violence compared to children growing up in the 1970s. And since our children are growing up in this environment, they are being strongly imprinted by these distorted and fearful messages.

A large part of the work I facilitate for my clients is to help them 'unhook' from what I like to refer to as the 'control drama' by challenging collective, fear-based perceptions that are influencing their limiting beliefs, perceptions and experiences. *Attachment Theory*, *Epigenetics*, *Pre* and *Perinatal Psychology* and *Trauma* research help to create a framework for understanding who we are and how we got here as well as provide a map to help guide us beyond the madness. The key is to be able find the courage to swim against the collective current.

Summary

❖ Attachment is the emotional bond that develops between a child and a primary caregiver and is the most important aspect of child development beginning at the moment of birth.

❖ Attachment is understood to be the basic human need for a child to have a safe and close relationship with a parent or primary caregiver.

❖ Secure attachment patterns are established when the parent(s) are responsive to the child's needs.

❖ Securely attached children end up being curious, independent, ego-resilient and successful in forming healthy relationship patterns which then persist into adulthood.

Schemas

Schemas are mental constructs that organize our experiences beginning at birth. They initially develop around concrete principles as we begin to interact with our external world and the individuals who inhabit it. In response to stimulus in our environment, *schemas* shape our perceptions and beliefs about reality by unconsciously using those principles to infer future probabilities. These future probabilities occur on many levels stemming from the concrete, action-oriented experiences of grouping related objects during early childhood and move towards more abstract properties, inferences, events and ideas in adolescence.

"The foot feels the foot when it feels the ground."   - Buddha -

I refer to *schemas* as our mental map or cognitive GPS which we unconsciously use at all times to successfully navigate our external world. Without this map, we would be unable to get out of bed, let alone walk out the front door. Getting out of bed and walking out the front door becomes possible from the first time we crawled off the couch and felt our feet touch the ground. At that moment our *schemas* began to develop around the understanding that we can count on having solid ground underneath our feet and the memory of that experience is recorded. As a result of that memory, we are able to successfully navigate our external world by unconsciously inferring that our feet will also touch solid ground when we crawl out of our strollers, step off the curb or walk down the stairs.

All of our unconscious assumptions, perceptions and beliefs about ourselves, our external world and those who inhabit it, are informed by our *schemas*. They are the interface between the cellular memories of our experiences and the beliefs and subsequent behaviors that stem from those experiences. Our *schemas* organize those experiences in such a way that allow us to take 'short-cuts' as we move through the world based on what we've come to understand we can count on; what we have inferred about our future experiences without even thinking about them.

During infancy and early childhood our *schemas* are constantly changing through an ongoing process of new experiences being successfully 'assimilated' into our pre-existing *schemas*. Those experiences are then 'accommodated' when the *schemas* are re-organized and modified to include those experiences.

This process of 'accommodation' has the individual continuously creating and recreating new theories that he or she relies on unconsciously to successfully navigate his or her external world. It can be as simple as coming to the understanding at the age of two that when Dad goes to work every morning Mom feeds me breakfast. As we get older, our *schemas* become more advanced and can also include more sophisticated theories such as it's not safe to interact with Dad when he comes home from work because he's been drinking.

Cognitive dissonance is the experience we have when interacting or engaging with stimulus or information from our environment that is incongruent with our pre-existing *schemas*. I reference this experience as being consistent with the oft-used expression 'mind-blowing'. 'Mind-blowing' experiences initiate a mental and emotional process in which we are attempting to create mental congruency and emotional equilibrium in response to something that is occurring in our external world that we have never personally experienced before and is outside the parameter of what we would have unconsciously inferred was possible.

This is what happened for all of us in 2001 as the horror of 9/11 unfolded before our very eyes as we sat in our respective living rooms or offices fixated on our computers and TV's. We struggled in disbelief to assimilate what was happening into our pre-existing *schemas*. The disequilibrium was so great in response to the unimaginable series of events that we were witnessing in real time that we went through a cascading series of disorienting and debilitating responses cognitively, physically and emotionally. In order to return to some state of equilibrium; we needed to re-organize our personal and collective *schemas* to include this experience, inferring that similar experiences could and would be possible in the future. While this process of assimilation and accommodation was happening, I remember feeling extremely dissociative and unable to process much at all; other than to connect to a very deep awareness that everything that I knew to be true and counted on as evidence that I was safe and secure was up for review somewhere in the very depths of my being.

This is why historical events such as Pearl Harbor, the assassinations of JFK, the massacre at Columbine, and the attacks of 9/11 are seared not only in our collective, conscious memories, but also at a much deeper, more archetypal level of personal, social and cultural identity. This is because, in those moments, the world as we knew it ceased to exist when everything that we thought we knew and could count on became far less predictable.

Our ability to re-organize and modify our *schemas* around stimulus that is beyond our ability to process or comprehend is vital in determining our capacity to function moving forward. In the absence of being able to accommodate challenging new stimuli, the potential for having your 'mind blown' increases. If this were a movie, it would be the scene in which the light bulbs start to 'pop' and the floor beneath your feet begins to 'buckle'. In the real world, it would be the moment in which a psychotic break or dissociation from reality occurs; both of which are common in response to unimaginable and unexpected trauma.

When we grow up in safe and secure environments, we are able to maintain a sense of equilibrium when assimilating new experiences into our pre-existing, *schemas* because these experiences are gentle enough that they ensure our sense of safety and security while affirming our right to exist.

However, when we live in an environment that is infused with unpredictable stress, chaos and abuse; we spend most of our time trying to restore balance to the cognitive disequilibrium that results in response to these chronic threats. This is achieved by replacing the current, outmoded *schemas* with more advanced and sophisticated *schemas*.

When our childhood experiences are gentle, we are able to develop more expansive world views in response to our environment becoming larger and less secure. The more secure our environments and attachments are growing up; the greater our ability will be to explore outside of the predictable safety and security of those environments, including what we were taught to believe was true about ourselves and the world we live in.

The quality of relationships we form with friends, colleagues and significant others are always a reflection of our *schemas* because they were formed around experiences we had growing up regarding what it looks and feels like when we love and care about someone. As you can imagine, these experiences can cover a very wide spectrum of expressions of love depending on how safe, secure and loving our childhood environments were.

If, during childhood, our primary caregiver became enmeshed with us in an unconscious attempt to get their emotional needs met in ways they were unable to while in relationship with themselves, their friends or significant others; our *schemas* would have developed around the unconscious belief that we exist for the sole purpose of ensuring the well-being of others. This, in turn, puts into motion all sorts of pre-determined outcomes, including the dysfunctional patterns inherent in our relationships and the need to constantly apologize or explain ourselves because it is understood at a very deep, unconscious level that our right to exist is always conditional on the well-being of others.

Whether concrete or abstract; our *schemas* develop in response to our curiosity with the external world and our desire to make sense of our experiences in order to ensure that everything in our lives is much more predictable.

The younger we are, the less developed our *schemas* are allowing us to be more fluid in response to whatever is occurring. This is when 'magical thinking' and creativity is at its fullest because we live in a world full of infinite possibilities.

Much of the healing I facilitate for myself and my clients is designed to re-organize and modify our *schemas* to include the awareness that we are fundamentally safe and secure even while living in an unpredictable world. From this awareness, we can now begin to successfully navigate our environment and the people who inhabit it from a place of unending curiosity and spontaneity; thereby increasing our capacity to experience love, joy and fulfillment in all that we do.

Summary

❖ *Schemas are mental constructs that organize our experiences beginning at birth.*

❖ *During infancy and early childhood our schemas are constantly changing through an ongoing process of new experiences being successfully 'assimilated' into our pre-existing schemas.*

❖ *Those experiences are then 'accommodated' when the schemas are re-organized and modified to include those experiences.*

❖ *In response to stimulus in our environment, schemas shape our perceptions and beliefs about reality by unconsciously using those principles to infer future probabilities.*

❖ *Our schemas are the interface between the cellular memories of our experiences and the beliefs and subsequent behaviors that stem from those experiences.*

Understanding Behaviors

Three of the most important things to understand about all behaviors; whether they are personal, professional, someone else's, our own, or being demonstrated by a child or adult:

1. *All behaviors make perfect sense when you understand the underlying schemas and imprints that influence them.*

2. *All behaviors are expressions of the individual unconsciously attempting to get their physical and emotional needs met.*

3. *Everyone, at any given moment, is showing up and doing their best.*

Understanding these three tenets allows us to move beyond the duality of our personal and professional relationships, including our own conditioning and subsequent imprinting.

So let's take a closer look to get a better understanding of what it is I'm referring to:

"All behaviors make perfect sense when you understand the underlying schemas and imprints that influence them."

When reviewing the role of schemas from the previous chapter, we are reminded that they act as our cognitive GPS which we unconsciously rely on to navigate our external world. Schemas develop throughout our most critical stages of development in response to our experiences and act as the interface between our cellular imprints and our perceptions of self, others and our external world. We unconsciously rely on our schemas to infer future probabilities, both concrete and abstract. In turn, these inferences become the motivation for all of our behaviors.

"All behaviors are expressions of the individual unconsciously attempting to get their physical and emotional needs met."

In addition to relying on our schemas to help us successfully navigate our external world at the concrete, rational level; we also rely on them to infer more abstract, future outcomes regarding how we can be reassured that our emotional needs will be met. These inferences are based on our previous relationships and experiences which began at the moment of conception when we were implanted in our very first environment and influenced by how securely we were attached to this environment and our primary caregivers. If our experiences throughout childhood were primarily safe and secure, and our primary caregivers were attentive to our needs; then our schemas would have developed in such a way that our behaviors would consistently reflect that level of stability. Dysfunctional, reactive and manipulative behaviors suggest significant trauma imprinting from stressful, chaotic and unsafe, childhood environments that end up being replicated throughout adulthood. Regardless of whether the behaviors are considered stable or maladaptive; they always reflect our best attempts, in the moment, to get our emotional needs met.

"Everyone, at any given moment, is showing up and doing their best."

I have found that this tenet is the hardest one for folks to accept because our schemas formed around extremely different conditioning and subsequent beliefs within the dualistic paradigm. We grew up with infinite projections that had us believe that we needed to keep trying harder in order to excel beyond our capacity in order to meet the expectations of others. Standardized learning became a big part of this conditioning, which often taught us that our best was never good enough as we were being measured against a standard that had very little to do with our own abilities and individual needs. Our best was often, if not always, being measured in relation to a larger collective and always by someone other than ourselves. This conditioning not only occurs within our personal relationships, but also from the larger collective of our cultural conditioning which reinforces our belief that in order to be loved and accepted we need to consistently achieve some level of excellence. This, in turn, guarantees that our emotional needs will be met through projections of positive regard and acceptance by others. In the absence of being able to achieve these external standards of perfection; we embody at the cellular/molecular level that we are not enough.

Within the dualistic paradigm, our inability to meet the expectation of others has always been evidence of us not doing our best because this is the paradigm in which we are always being reflected back to ourselves by the other. However, these projections are also unconscious attempts by others to minimize their own anxiety relative to whatever imprinting and subsequent beliefs they are unconsciously holding on to which constantly identifies that they are not enough; and so on, and so on, and so on....

Whatever we choose to do at any given moment is what we think is best until we have a different understanding of what that is. Once have a different understanding of what that is; we choose that instead. Our degree of mental and emotional stability combined with our level of awareness, at any given moment, will always determine what that looks like.

If we are able to accept the tenet that everyone, at any given moment, is showing up and doing their best; then we have allowed ourselves to step beyond the duality of our own conditioning. The ability to do so dissolves our own imprinting and subsequent self-judgments that has us believing that we are not enough because we are finally able to accept that we have always shown up and done our best, without exception. For those of us who engage in 'life reviews' from time to time and continue to cringe at whatever our version of 'best' was ten years ago, three years ago, or even six months ago; it is important to remember that the tendency to cringe is evidence that we continue to grow and develop and increase our awareness. This is always a cause for celebration rather than self-recrimination.

Many factors influence what that might look like including our age/schematic development, our environment, our history of abuse/neglect/trauma and whatever we may have inherited through our respective DNA lineages. Any of these factors makes us vulnerable to manifest some emotional, mental or physical imbalance/disease expression in response to whatever stressors we've experienced throughout the course of our lifetime.

When sitting with clients, I often refer to the extreme as an example to illustrate new concepts within this new paradigm of thinking; beyond the duality of our conditioning:

On July 20, 2012, James Holmes walked into an Aurora, Colorado movie theater and using two tear gas grenades, a Smith & Wesson M&P15 rifle, a Remington 870 Express Tactical shotgun, and a Glock 22 handgun; he shot and killed 12 people while injuring 70 others. At that moment, James Holmes was doing his best. At that moment, his mind was literally falling apart. His mental constructs had broken down to the extent that this unimaginable, premeditated act of violence made complete sense to him. It had to; otherwise he wouldn't have done it. Had his mind not been falling apart, his best would have looked remarkably different and there would not have been such unimaginable and unexpected loss of life and trauma in an environment that his victims had every reason to believe was safe.

Having worked with individuals whose mental constructs have broken down; it's probably much easier for me to accept this tenet. However, if you just allow yourself to sit with it for longer than a minute or two, the simple logic of such a concept is self-evident and will begin to make sense. What makes it difficult to accept 'at first glance' is that our collective conditioning keeps reinforcing the duality and subsequent belief that we should have the ability to control 'bad' things from happening to 'good' people in an attempt to reassure ourselves that we could never become victims of such horrific acts of violence; or that someone we know and love could ever perpetrate such unimaginable carnage.

Unfortunately, there are far too many examples showing up in this country and around the world every day that makes it impossible to guarantee our safety and security from individuals whose 'best' can change the course of many lives in just a few minutes, resulting in unimaginable suffering no matter how hard we try to anticipate and control their behaviors.

All behaviors, including maladaptive behaviors, are outward expressions of our cellular imprinting and subsequent schemas. Therefore, it is ineffective to focus exclusively on the behavior as an intervention in an attempt to influence a different outcome. When we do so, as expressed through the current models of the mental health, academic, political and legal systems; we limit the potential for any significant change to occur. Chemically restraining, physically incarcerating, or putting to death individuals as a means of controlling and containing what it is that makes us feel uncomfortable and unsafe will always ensure that in the absence of these external control mechanisms; the behaviors will persist. Significant, long-term change for individuals and society, as a whole, requires a much deeper inquiry at the cellular level.

Summary

❖ *All behaviors make perfect sense when you understand the underlying schemas and imprints that influence them.*

❖ *All behaviors are expressions of the individual unconsciously attempting to get their physical and emotional needs met.*

❖ *Everyone, at any given moment, is showing up and doing their best.*

Parenting the Child

Despite this being a large and comprehensive topic in the field of human development; all of the work that I have facilitated for children and their families during the past eleven years, as well as my own experience as a parent, has helped me distill my primary focus down to one specific tenet regarding childhood development.

Joseph Chilton Pearce described it best in 1977 in his groundbreaking book, *"Magical Child"*:

"Learning to take our cues from the child and make a corresponding response means learning to heed and respond to the primary process in ourselves as well. A child can teach us an incredible amount if we are willing to learn, and because s/he is biologically geared to take his/her cues from us, s/he learns as we do."

I believe that it is the most important dynamic to embrace and embody for parents who seek to model and demonstrate positive, loving and healthy relationship patterns for their children. In doing so, the greatest opportunity for the child to know themselves and actualize their fullest potential is achieved.

Unfortunately, cultural conditioning over countless generations has created very different relationship dynamics within the familial, academic and community environments. Conformity to whatever agenda the prevailing authority figure(s) has determined is appropriate for the child and society, as a whole, is achieved and reinforced through a system of punishments and rewards.

The problem with this approach is that all that has been accomplished is to 'bend' the child to the will, boundaries and false limitations of whoever is 'in charge'. Not only is the wound/trauma imprinting reinforced in the adult who takes this approach, but it subsequently creates similar wound/trauma imprinting in the child. Consequently, the child and the adult become imprisoned together within these limiting, shaming and fear-based beliefs because the parents are only at ease when the child is able, and willing, to conform to whatever conditions and limitations are being placed on them.

"No matter how we camouflage our intent, to ourselves and to our child, all parenting and education is based on: "Do this or you will suffer the consequences." This threat underlies every facet of our life from our first potty training through university exams, doctoral candidate's orals, employment papers, income tax, on and on ad infinitum down to official death. Culture is a massive exercise in restraint, inhibiting, and curtailment of joy on behalf of pseudo and grim necessities."

— Joseph Chilton Pearce, "The Biology of Transcendence" —

Children enter the world with the capacity for optimal growth and development. However, well-meaning parents begin to limit and distort this capacity from the moment they become aware that another life has been conceived and they begin to project identifications on to the child that have nothing to do with the unique being who is taking shape and form in the mother's womb. After the child is born, these projections continue well into adulthood since most parents believe that they have a responsibility as 'guide' and 'teacher' to bestow onto their child all of what they believe to be true about them, the external world, and 'reality' in general.

What they fail to recognize, however, is that their well-meaning attempts to be responsible and effective parents has more to do with their own agendas than it does the child's best interests. This is because their ideas about parenting are always being informed by their own unconscious and unresolved wound imprinting and subsequent, fear-based, beliefs from childhood.

"Since we must pattern ourselves and our worldview after our culture and parents, when that is a disordered system for modeling, we are ourselves disordered in precisely the same way."

- Joseph Chilton Pearce, "Bond of Power" -

I have never met a parent, including myself, who was not somehow trying to compensate for how they were parented during their own childhood when determining their specific style of parenting. Unfortunately, it turns out, that when we parent from our unresolved wounding in an attempt to ensure that our children are not wounded in the manner or to the degree that we were; we end up just shifting to the opposite end of the spectrum and are as equally out of balance as we judged our parents to be.

Shifting this parenting paradigm requires that we be open to learning new patterns and possibilities; the absence of which has us responding and reacting from unconscious defense mechanisms stemming from whatever wounding we, as parents, experienced throughout our own childhoods and still carry with us in the form of cellular imprinting and limiting beliefs. This shift requires a tremendous amount of trust which is counter-intuitive to the control dynamics that we were raised with and have relied on to ensure our own survival at the deepest levels.

It is extremely challenging for a parent to trust that their child carries an inherent, intuitive understanding of who they are and what they came here to do and that their role, as a parent, has less to do with being a mechanism for control and instruction, and more to do with being a loving reflection of acceptance, acknowledgment and reassurance. It is this dynamic, and only this dynamic, that creates the safest and most secure environment for the child to explore their world, develop their identity, and actualize their fullest potential.

What makes it so difficult to model is that the parent is encoded with cellular memory that continuously identifies that the world is not safe and in response to their anxiety around this distorted belief; utilizes external control mechanisms in order to ensure that their child is safe. Unfortunately, these fear-based, control dynamics accomplish very little other than to infuse the child with the same level of anxiety that the parent is vibrating around.

Since a large part of human development is about ongoing identity formation; it's important to bring awareness and understanding to the fact that a child growing up in a controlled, anxious and fearful environment will have an extremely limited opportunity to explore and identify their true sense of self. Taking cues from this type of environment leaves the child no other option other than to learn, from a very early age, the importance of being able to defend them self. This posture is then reinforced throughout their lifetime and reflected in all of their relationship dynamics. Therefore, a very different parenting paradigm is required in order to have the desired impact on human development; a paradigm that is no longer being determined by the parent's fear-based, agendas or self-interests, but is reciprocal in meeting the true needs of both the child and the adult.

Decision-making and behavioral expressions are primarily shaped and determined by the anticipated response the child has learned to expect from those individuals who have the greatest control and influence over them. Therefore, I am always reminding the parents I work with to stop telling their children who they are and what they need to do and to just join them, in the moment, in their experience.

However, children whose parents continue to have the perception that their child is out of control, are just reflections of how much the parent needs to be in control in order to feel safe and secure. This has nothing to do with the child, but is rather a reflection of the parent's own conditioning and unresolved imprinting from childhood. It is for this reason that I always, without exception, choose to work as much with the parent(s) as I do the child.

"Once shame is imprinted there will never again be "unquestioned acceptance of the given" but a faltering hesitancy as doubt intrudes and clouds the child's knowledge of self and world"

- Joseph Chilton Pearce, "The Biology of Transcendence"-

Letting go of the unconscious agendas that infuse the child's environment and shape their limiting beliefs about themselves and their world is paramount in ensuring that they have the potential to realize themselves without shame or self-recrimination.

Once again:

"Learning to take our cues from the child and make a corresponding response means learning to heed and respond to the primary process in ourselves as well. A child can teach us an incredible amount if we are willing to learn, and because s/he is biologically geared to take his/her cues from us, s/he learns as we do."

- Joseph Chilton Pearce, "Magical Child" -

A paradigm such as this takes us all beyond the duality of our cultural conditioning and childhood imprinting by providing new patterns and possibilities for anyone who mentors, teaches, parents or works with children; thereby changing the course of human development for future generations.

Summary

❖ *Parenting styles are always being influenced by the parent's own unconscious and unresolved wound imprinting and fear-based, beliefs from childhood.*

❖ *Well-meaning attempts to be responsible and effective parents have more to do with the parent's unconscious agendas than it has to do with the child's best interests.*

❖ *Conformity to whatever agenda the prevailing authority figure has determined is appropriate for the child is achieved and reinforced through a system of punishments and rewards.*

❖ *The problem with this approach is that all that has been accomplished is to 'bend' the child to the will, boundaries and false limitations of whoever is 'in charge'.*

❖ *The child and the adult become imprisoned together within these limiting, shaming, and fear-based patterns and beliefs because the parents are only at ease when the child is able and willing to conform to whatever conditions and limitations are being placed on them.*

❖ *Children enter the world with the capacity for optimal growth and development*

❖ *Learning to take our cues from the child and make a corresponding response means learning to heed and respond to the primary process in ourselves as well.*

❖ *A child can teach us an incredible amount if we are willing to learn, and because s/he is biologically geared to take his/her cues from us, s/he learns as we do.*

Adolescence

ADOLESCENCE

❖ As children develop, they begin to model the existential angst that comes from their inability to conform to the conditioning inherent within the paradigm of our social and cultural conditioning.

❖ It begins with emerging adolescence and the dawn of meta-cognition when the individual begins to experience conformity as an equivalent to death.

❖ Without realizing it; they are defending their right to exist beyond the boundaries and confinement of this conditioning that projects onto them that their inability to conform is evidence of some inherent flaw that will limit their ability to be successful in getting their physical and emotional needs met throughout the course of their lifetime.

❖ What is being reflected back to them from their environments is negating them and challenging their ability to be in integrity with themselves in response to the distorted messages and unrealistic expectations being projected onto them.

❖ *Adolescence trying to function within the paradigm of this conditioning is a perfect storm which is why this stage of development is often defined by drama and crisis.*

❖ *If we, as adults, were able to recognize the degree to which we are influenced by our own imprinting and subsequent conditioning; we would be much better equipped to parent, teach and mentor this most critical and dynamic stage of development.*

❖ *Our teenagers are our 'truth tellers' and we have much to learn from them if we could only allow ourselves to listen and accept them without feeling the need to defend our position.*

The Dualistic Paradigm

A paradigm is a framework which contains widely accepted beliefs and perceptions about reality. Participation in any paradigm by the collective mainstream is happening at an unconscious level as a result of chronic conditioning that begins from the moment we are born. The dualistic paradigm is the current, collective framework that almost every sentient being on this planet participates in unconsciously every day.

Duality occurs when it is perceived that two aspects of something are separate from, and in opposition to, each other. All of our schemas from the moment of birth have developed around the conditioning of this binary state of mutual exclusion. It informs all of our perceptions and beliefs about ourselves and our environment, and because these beliefs determine our expectations; our external world continues to reflect back to us that we are separate from, and in opposition to, everything that exists outside of us.

Thousands of years ago, earth-centered cultures lived in harmony with the natural world because their inherent cosmologies and subsequent creation stories identified that they were an integral part of their environment; no greater and no less than a rock, a tree, a mountain, a bird, a deer or a spider. Everything they did, including relationships, ceremonies, government and education reflected this central theme. As a result, concepts such as balance, integrity, respect, reverence, and gratitude were easily embodied and as natural as breathing. Inclusion, rather than exclusion, was a way of being that permeated the individual on a cellular level and influenced behaviors, relationship dynamics and one's overall quality of life, which was imbued with a sense of purpose and belonging.

Historians and philosophers believe that dualism originated only a few centuries ago through the Cartesian/philosophical and Newtonian/scientific view of the Universe, and that prior to the cosmologies that developed from these mechanistic worldviews; we experienced 'thinking' and 'being' as identical. Descartes's famous quote, "Cogito ergo sum"/"I think, therefore I am", identifies the fundamental split between consciousness that *thinks* and consciousness that *exists*. Within such a paradigm, we, as a species, have developed the ideology that mind and cognition are self-evident of our superiority to all other life forms on this planet and that those life forms exist solely for the purpose of sustaining us on a physical, emotional and spiritual level. These mechanistic and dualistic cosmologies have led to the exaltation of the human and our increasing alienation from the natural world which continues to influence our need to have dominion over it by excavating, controlling, manipulating and exhausting all of our natural resources. What has now become self-evident is that our continued participation in, and conformation to, the dualistic paradigm, propels us closer towards self-destruction.

Good/Bad, Right/Wrong, Heaven/Hell, Love/Hate, Pass/Fail, True/False, Black/White, Life/Death, Sane/Insane and *Masculine/Feminine* are just some of the dualities that reflect our participation in this binary state of mutual exclusion. Competition, dogma, opposition, poverty, exclusion, control, disparity, identity, hierarchy, conflict, manipulation, violence, and excess are all expressions of the dualistic paradigm and inform all of the pain, suffering and separation we experience in ourselves, our loved ones and our communities.

The perception of separation is the seed of all suffering and sets us up to participate in, and be conditioned by, the *Dualistic Paradigm* or, as I like to call it, *The Control Drama*. This existential sense of being separate from everything that we perceive exists outside of us is always being determined by our awareness that our time in this body and on this planet is finite. We are the only organisms that have this awareness and it sets us up to focus primarily on either the past that no longer exists or the future that hasn't happened yet. Without this awareness there would be no such thing as emotional instability or mental illness because all of the distortions we experience that inform these various expressions, including anxiety and depression, come from our unconscious attempts to mitigate loss by grasping at, and holding tightly to, whatever and whomever makes us feel safe and secure.

All of our wounding and trauma is perpetuated by others as we grow from infancy through vulnerable and critical stages of development in environments that reflect the chronic fear and anxiety that stems from these survival issues. As a result, our schemas develop around unconscious beliefs that include the need to control or be controlled in order to feel safe and secure.

Throughout history, man-made dogma has been expressed through all organized religions as a means of controlling large populations of people through fear and threats of punishment in the afterlife in the event that we are unable to conform to the current model of man-made, moral or ethical codes. Those of us who are compliant are promised unimaginable rewards. Within the dualistic paradigm these different outcomes of reward and punishment are usually experienced as love and acceptance or judgment and rejection while embodied, and referred to as some version of heaven or hell in the after-life. Consequently, conformity would seem to be the key to survival while spontaneity appears to be a dangerous course of action.

As a child and family therapist, I am always aware of how this deeply internalized paradigm manifests within the systems that have been put in place to address the mental, emotional and physical needs of the individual navigating every stage of development throughout the span of a lifetime. I notice it mostly because they don't appear to be particularly effective if the individual is not conforming to an increasingly narrow bandwidth of what would meet the current criteria of 'acceptable' or 'normal'. Remember, the *Dualistic Paradigm* is, by its very nature, exclusive; so if you don't conform then the reflexive response is a collective projection identifying that you suffer from either immoral, criminal or pathological tendencies. Once that happens; there is usually an attempt to restrain the individual either chemically with medication or physically with incarceration. This would explain why 49 million Americans are currently taking psychiatric medication and why the United States has now incarcerated 2.2 million of its citizens; a 500% increase in the past thirty years.

The most obvious example of this conditioning can be seen in the experiences of our children, from pre-K through high school, attempting to navigate the current academic system. What I find most intriguing is that as the child develops; he or she begins to model the existential angst that comes from their inability to conform to the dualistic conditioning inherent in this particular system. It begins with emerging adolescence and the dawn of meta-cognition when the individual begins to experience conformity as an equivalent to death. Without realizing it; they are defending their right to exist beyond the boundaries and the confinement of the dualistic paradigm that projects onto them that their inability to conform is evidence of some inherent flaw that will limit their ability to be successful in getting their needs met throughout the course of their lifetime.

The reason why I am able to relate so well to this demographic is because I understand what's occurring in their environment that is negating them and challenging their ability to be in integrity with themselves; in response to the distorted messages and unrealistic expectations that are being projected onto them daily by administrators, teachers and parents. It's amazing to experience the deep sighs of relief and increased engagement in response to having reflected back to them that there's nothing wrong with them; that they're not freaks, and they just need to learn how to successfully navigate their environments in a way that does not have them feeling diminished or negated. Adolescence trying to function within the dualistic paradigm is a perfect storm, which is why this developmental stage is primarily defined by drama and crisis. If we, as adults, were able to recognize the degree to which we've conformed to our own conditioning; we would be much better equipped to parent, teach and mentor them. Our teenagers are our 'truth tellers' and we have much to learn from them if we could only allow ourselves to listen and accept them without feeling the need to defend ourselves.

The good news is that it appears as if a much more holistic paradigm of consciousness has begun to emerge and that, once again, the scientific model of the time is reflecting these new beliefs and shifting paradigms. Quantum Physics is beginning to replace the mechanistic view of Newtonian Physics and is teaching us with every new discovery that we are intimately interconnected with our environment and everything that inhabits it. This also includes the understanding that we can change what is outside of us by simply changing ourselves. Much of this awareness is an integral part of what has guided my own healing process as well as informed the healing that I am able to facilitate for my clients. As long as we are oriented to looking outside of ourselves in order to identify what or who, in our environment, is causing us pain; we will always be trying to manipulate and control our environment in an attempt to minimize our suffering.

In order to be balanced, whole and healthy; we must move beyond the conditioning that has taught us that we are separate and apart from anything that we perceive exists outside of us. In order to move beyond this dualistic orientation that has us stuck in the identity of victimhood; we must be able to embrace inclusion, beginning with ourselves. It is critical that our attention be directed primarily inward, towards the self, to heal whatever judgments we defend against that reinforce the internal 'splits' and subsequent fear and anxiety that is informing all of our personal and professional relationships, including our relationship with the self.

If more of us were able to engage in a self-exhaustive process of healing the imprinting and subsequent 'splits' we hold deeply at the cellular level and defend daily; we would then be able to move beyond the fear-based expressions of the dualistic paradigm. Competition, opposition, exclusion, control, disparity, conflict, manipulation, violence and excess would then be replaced with cooperation, inclusion, balance, acceptance, integrity, respect, reverence, love and gratitude.

If we were able to heal ourselves at the cellular level; our external world would then begin to reflect back to us this internal paradigm shift, resulting in all of our perceptions, behaviors and relationship dynamics being imbued with a renewed sense of balance, purpose and well-being.

Summary

❖ *A paradigm is a framework which contains widely accepted beliefs and perceptions about reality.*

❖ *The dualistic paradigm is the current, collective framework that almost every sentient being on this planet participates in unconsciously every day.*

❖ *Duality occurs when it is perceived that two aspects of something are separate from, and in opposition to, each other.*

❖ *All of our schemas from the moment of birth have developed around the conditioning of this binary state of mutual exclusion.*

❖ *It influences all of our perceptions and beliefs about our self, others and our environment.*

❖ *Because these beliefs shape our expectations; our external world continues to reflect back to us that we are separate from, and in opposition to, everything that exists outside of us.*

❖ *This existential sense of being separate from everything that we perceive exists outside of us is always being determined by our awareness that our time in this body and on this planet is finite.*

❖ *Without this awareness there would be no such thing as emotional instability or mental illness because all of the distortions we experience that inform these various expressions, including anxiety and depression, come from our unconscious attempts to mitigate loss by grasping at and holding tightly to whatever and whomever makes us feel safe and secure.*

❖ *All of our wounding and trauma is perpetuated by others as we grow from infancy through vulnerable and critical stages of development in environments that reflect the chronic fear and anxiety that stems from these survival issues.*

❖ *Our schemas then develop around unconscious beliefs that include the need to control or be controlled in order to feel safe and secure.*

What is Normal?

"The aim of Western psychiatry is to help the troubled individual to adjust himself to the society of less troubled individuals who are observed to be well adjusted to one another and the local institutions, but about whose adjustment to the Fundamental Order of Things no inquiry is made. Counseling, analysis, and other methods of therapy are used to bring these troubled and maladjusted persons back to a normality, which is defined, for lack of any better criterion, in statistical terms. To be normal is to be a member of the majority party - or in totalitarian societies, such as Calvinist Geneva, Nazi Germany, Communist Russia, of the party that happens to be in power. History and anthropology make it abundantly clear that societies composed of individuals who think, feel, believe and act according to the most preposterous conventions can survive for long periods of time. Statistical normality is perfectly compatible with a high degree of folly and wickedness. But there is another kind of normality - a normality of perfect functioning, a normality of actualized potentialities, a normality of nature in its fullest flower. This normality has nothing to do with the observed behavior of the greatest number - for the greatest number live, and have always lived, with their potentialities unrealized, their nature denied its full development."   - Alduous Huxley -

As a mental health professional advocating for children, adolescents and their families within the legal, academic and social institutions for a number of years; I have observed a growing intolerance within our society for behavioral presentations and patterns that do not conform to an increasingly narrow perception of what is 'normal'. Simultaneous to this increasing intolerance is a continuous breakdown within the institutions themselves; which limits their ability to respond effectively to the needs of the individual.

Unprecedented cutbacks in education, arts and social programs which assist our most vulnerable citizens; the young, the elderly, the impoverished and the disabled; have created a new culture of 'normal', one in which our ability to respond to the 'troubled' or 'maladapted' individual is becoming more and more limited to chemical restraints.

In our public schools, physical exercise, creative expression and critical thinking skills have been replaced with educational strategies such as *No Child Left Behind* and *Standards of Learning* requirements that entrain our children to focus primarily on test-taking and grade percentages; the results of which appear to directly correlate to their developing sense of self-worth or lack thereof.

Policies such as *Zero Tolerance* have created a fear-based culture of reactivity within our academic institutions; resulting in extreme, irrational consequences for what was previously recognized as falling within the spectrum of developmentally appropriate behaviors.

Consequently, we are now engaged in the largest social experiment in history in which we believe that it makes perfect sense to chemically restrain our children when their behaviors and achievements do not conform to our individual and collective expectations. As of 2013, IMS Health, best known for its collection of health care information, reported in their national database that 8,389,034 children in the U.S. between the ages of 0 and 17 were taking psychiatric medication.

These children are receiving pharmacological interventions despite the absence of longitudinal studies that have *not* been funded by pharmaceutical companies excluding long-term, negative consequences on a brain still in its formative stages of development. It would seem that the widespread practice of chemically restraining our young citizens ensures their 'survival' now that they can adjust more easily to the *Fundamental Order of Things* of which, clearly, no serious inquiry is being made.

Summary

❖ *A growing intolerance continues within our society to behavioral presentations and patterns that do not conform to an increasingly narrow and fear-based perception of what is 'normal'.*

❖ *Decreased funding within the institutions that assist our most vulnerable citizens; the young, the elderly, the impoverished and the disabled, has created a new culture of 'normal'; one in which our ability to respond to the 'troubled' or 'maladapted' individual is becoming more and more limited to chemical restraints.*

❖ *We are now engaged in the largest social experiment in history in which we believe that it makes perfect sense to chemically restrain our children when their behaviors and achievements do not conform to our expectations.*

❖ *There are no longitudinal studies that have **not** been funded by pharmaceutical companies excluding long-term, negative consequences on a brain still in its formative stages of development.*

Locus of Control

Julian B. Rotter was an American psychologist who developed the *Social Learning Theory* in 1954 which identified that an individual's behavior was largely influenced by environmental factors within a social context. This was a departure from earlier theories based on psychoanalysis, which identified behaviors as being driven primarily by psychological factors.

Rotter theorized that negative and positive outcomes were largely responsible for determining if an individual was likely to repeat a behavior. As the framework for his *Social Learning Theory*, he further developed the understanding of *Locus of Control* which attempted to differentiate between two concepts which he referred to as 'achievement motivation' (*Internal Locus of Control*) and 'outer-directedness' (*External Locus of Control*). He attributed these two different concepts as aspects of the individual's personality in determining the extent to which people believe they can control events affecting them. This was measured on a scale which he referred to as a continuum in which individuals either believed outcomes in their lives were attributed to their own abilities (*Internal Locus of Control*) or to chance, luck or destiny (*External Locus of Control*). Rotter's theories were grounded in the fields of *Social* and *Personality Psychology.*

My interpretation and application of *Locus of Control* is slightly different than I believe Rotter had intended. How I interpret it applies primarily to the field of *Developmental Psychology.*

Throughout the stages of childhood development, our behaviors are primarily being shaped and determined by outside influences which include our primary caregivers, siblings, teachers, coaches, grandparents and babysitters. Negative consequences and positive reinforcements are designed to reinforce the behaviors which are considered more acceptable and discourage those that are not. Over time we learn that the most effective way to get our physical and emotional needs met is to behave in ways that elicit the greatest amount of acknowledgment, acceptance, positive regard and love from others. The developmental stages of childhood and early adolescence are largely influenced by what Rotter would refer to as 'outer-directedness' or *External Locus of Control.* Decision-making and behavioral expressions are primarily shaped and determined by the anticipated response the child has learned to expect from those individuals in their environment who have the greatest control and influence on them.

As the child grows into adolescence, a hallmark of this developmental stage is 'increased differentiation' from the very people in their environment who have had the greatest influence in shaping their schemas and subsequent beliefs and behaviors. It is my contention that the adolescent's ability to successfully navigate from this developmental stage into adulthood is largely determined by their ability to shift from 'outer-directedness' or *External Locus of Control* to 'achievement motivation' or *Internal Locus of Control*. However, despite this shift being optimal in determining a healthy transition into adulthood; it often puts the adolescent on a collision course with the very individuals in their environment who have had the greatest influence on them since birth.

Increased differentiation from our parents is a requirement for transitioning successfully into adulthood. However, in order for this to happen, the parents or primary caregivers need to be fairly healthy, balanced, conscious and aware. If they are not, then they will take the child's attempts to differentiate from them very personally. They experience it as extremely threatening since their influence and control over their child appears to be diminishing. This is evidenced by the fact that the negative consequences and positive reinforcements that they have come to rely on to elicit acceptable behaviors in their child are no longer effective. In response to this unwelcome development, the parent usually ratchets up the control mechanisms and engages in increased power struggles with their child which always fail to satisfy either party's needs.

Whenever I get the opportunity to work with parents before their child reaches adolescence; I make sure I spend a significant amount of time on the subject of *External Locus of Control* vs. *Internal Locus of Control*. *Locus of Control* is as an unconscious mechanism that continues to influence how we attempt to get our physical and emotional needs met throughout our entire lifespan. It is my assertion that being able to shift that mechanism from an external orientation to an internal one during adolescence is critical in ensuring that we mature into healthy, self-reliant adults who are successful in getting their needs met.

I do not believe, as Rotter theorized, that the tendency to operate from either *Internal* or *External Locus of Control* is a personality trait that is crystallized throughout the individual's life span. Instead, I believe that the pattern of relying on the self or the environment to determine our behaviors is a byproduct of our imprinting and conditioning within our childhood environments as we continued to develop around the need to have our emotional and physical needs met. Once we accept that premise then we can accept that the tendency to be over-reliant on others to reassure us that we are performing and behaving appropriately can shift even in adulthood once we bring conscious awareness to the pattern.

Being in alignment and integrity with the self requires that we mature beyond the *External Locus of Control* orientation in which the need to conform to the expectations of others and our social conditioning is the primary motivation for getting our physical and emotional needs met. An over-reliance on others to influence our perceptions, beliefs and behaviors well into adulthood suggests chronic imprinting from a controlling, childhood environment largely influenced by fear and anxiety. In the absence of those external controls, we are unable to mature as adults into the *Internal Locus of Control* orientation because we were never able to develop that mechanism before launching ourselves into the world.

So rather than think of *Internal* and *External Locus of Control* as the difference between believing whether or not you have control over events in your life; I encourage you to think of it more as the difference between whether or not you rely primarily on yourself or others to determine the choices you make in life including how you attempt to get your physical and emotional needs met.

Summary

❖ *Throughout the stages of childhood development, our behaviors are primarily being shaped and determined by outside influences which include our primary caregivers, siblings, teachers, coaches, grandparents and babysitters.*

❖ *Over time, we learn that the most effective way to get our physical and emotional needs met is to behave in ways that elicit the greatest amount of acceptance, positive regard and love from others.*

❖ *Decision-making and behavioral expressions are primarily shaped and determined by the anticipated response the child has learned to expect from those individuals in their environment who have the greatest control and influence on them.*

❖ *The developmental stages of childhood and early adolescence are largely influenced by 'outer-directedness' or External Locus of Control.*

❖ *The adolescent's ability to successfully navigate from this developmental stage into adulthood is largely determined by their ability to shift from 'outer-directedness' or External Locus of Control to 'achievement motivation' or Internal Locus of Control.*

❖ *Despite this shift being optimal in determining a healthy transition into adulthood; it often puts the adolescent on a collision course with the individuals in their environment which have had the greatest influence on them since they were born.*

❖ *Being in alignment and integrity with the self requires that we mature beyond the External Locus of Control orientation in which the need to conform to the expectations of others and our social conditioning is the primary motivation for getting our physical and emotional needs met.*

Parenting the Adolescence

Adolescence is the most complex and challenging stage of development an individual will ever have to navigate. Rapid physical, hormonal and neuronal changes are occurring every day, resulting in increased vulnerability to environmental stressors which can often result in emotional and behavioral issues manifesting as a defense mechanism to those perceived stressors. Depression, substance abuse, anxiety, suicidal ideation, truancy, cutting and increased oppositional defiance are just some of the issues that can manifest as coping mechanisms in response to this increased psychological and physiological vulnerability.

An additional reinforcement to the potential instability of adolescence is the emergence of newly sophisticated metacognitive abilities which lead to increased egocentrism, self-absorption and the development of *The Personal Fable*. *The Personal Fable* is the view of the adolescent that what happens to them is unique, exceptional and shared by no one else. They may feel that no one has ever experienced the pain they feel, that no one has ever been treated so badly, or that no one can understand what they are going through. This perceptual framework can lead to feelings of isolation, despair and disconnect; further increasing the adolescent's vulnerability to manifest maladaptive behaviors.

During the time my son was navigating the challenges of this complex developmental stage; I was compelled to make myself a T-shirt with the following inscription on it:

Mothers of teenagers understand why wolves eat their young

What made this sentiment even more apropos was that, at the time, we were living in the Adirondacks with wolves. So we were both able to enjoy the sentiment with the provision that I not wear it out in public while in his company.

All of my experiences, both personal and professional, have helped me discern over the years that the most balanced and effective approach to parenting the adolescent is achieved by focusing primarily on what it means to be an adolescent from the perspective of the adolescent.

Joining the adolescent where they happen to be in the moment, in their experience, is the most important thing we can do. This requires that we, as parents, teachers and mentors, suspend our own personal agendas in favor of establishing a truly empathic connection with the teenager. What makes this difficult to do is that the adolescent's experience is often infused with a lot of instability, drama and crisis;

which serves as a reflection and painful reminder for all of us of a time in which we experienced the same deep existential angst and suffering that often defines this critical stage of development.

In addition to not wanting to revisit our own imprinting from adolescence; parents will become extremely uncomfortable with the recognition that they have less influence on their child than in previous years despite using the same external control mechanisms which had always proven successful. So what has changed?

Around the age of twelve, rapid neuronal changes in the brain result in newly emerging metacognitive abilities. Metacognition is essentially 'thinking about thinking', and once the adolescent has reached this cognitive benchmark; from their perspective, everything is up for review, including whether or not they will continue to conform to the conditioning and control mechanisms that have been in place since they were born.

Once again, from the chapter, *"Locus of Control"*:

"As the child grows into adolescence, a hallmark of this developmental stage is increased differentiation from the very people in their environment who have had the greatest influence in shaping their schemas and subsequent beliefs and behaviors. It is my contention that the adolescent's ability to successfully navigate from this developmental stage into adulthood is largely determined by their ability to shift from 'outer-

directedness' or External Locus of Control to 'achievement motivation' or Internal Locus of Control. However, despite this shift being optimal in determining a healthy transition into adulthood; it often puts the adolescent on a collision course with the individuals in their environment which have had the greatest influence on them since they were born."

"Increased differentiation from our parents is a requirement for transitioning successfully into adulthood. However, in order for this to happen, the parents or primary caregivers need to be fairly healthy, balanced, conscious and aware. If they are not, then they will take the child's attempts to differentiate from them very personally. They experience it as extremely threatening since their influence and control over their child appears to be diminishing. This is evidenced by the fact that the negative consequences and positive reinforcements that they have come to rely on to elicit acceptable behaviors in their child are no longer effective. In response to this unwelcome development, the parent usually ratchets up the control mechanisms and engages in increased power struggles with their child which always fails to satisfy either party's needs."

One of my many mantras to the parents I work with is "Don't get involved in a power struggle with your teenager." It is my experience that if you do, you will always lose because the adolescent is often willing to take them self off the planet rather than conform to control mechanisms which, for them, represent the equivalent of self-annihilation.

"Without realizing it; they are defending their right to exist beyond the boundaries and confinement of this conditioning that projects onto them that their inability to conform is evidence of some inherent flaw that will limit their ability to be successful in getting their physical and emotional needs met throughout the course of their lifetime." - Beyond the Imprint -

What is most important for the parent to understand is that their control/defense mechanisms are more of an attempt to get their own physical and emotional needs met by alleviating the anxiety associated with the increasing awareness that they fundamentally have very little, if any, control over their teenager who is striving for greater autonomy and independence.

"If we, as adults, were able to recognize the degree to which we are influenced by our own imprinting and subsequent conditioning; we would be much better equipped to parent, teach and mentor this most critical and dynamic stage of developmental. Our teenagers are our 'truth tellers' and we have much to learn from them if we could only allow ourselves to listen and accept them without feeling the need to defend our position." - Beyond the Imprint -

Summary

❖ *Adolescence is the most complex and challenging stage of development an individual will ever have to navigate.*

❖ *Rapid physical, hormonal and neuronal changes are occurring every day, resulting in increased vulnerability to environmental stressors which can often result in emotional and behavioral issues manifesting as defense mechanisms to those perceived stressors.*

❖ *The most balanced and effective approach to parenting the adolescent is achieved by focusing primarily on what it means to be an adolescent from the perspective of the adolescent.*

❖ *Joining the adolescent where they happen to be in the moment, in their experience, is the most important thing we can do.*

❖ *This requires that parents, teachers and mentors, suspend their own agendas in favor of establishing a truly empathic connection with the teenager.*

❖ *Parents will become extremely uncomfortable with the recognition that they have less influence on their child than in previous years, despite using the same external control mechanisms which had always proven successful.*

❖ *What is most important for the parent to understand is that their control/defense mechanisms are more of an attempt to get their own physical and emotional needs met by alleviating the anxiety associated with the increasing awareness that they fundamentally have very little, if any, control over their teenager.*

❖ *Don't get involved in a power struggle with your teenager because if you do, you will always lose.*

❖ *Our teenagers are our 'truth tellers' and we have much to learn from them if we could only allow ourselves to listen and accept them without feeling the need to defend our position.*

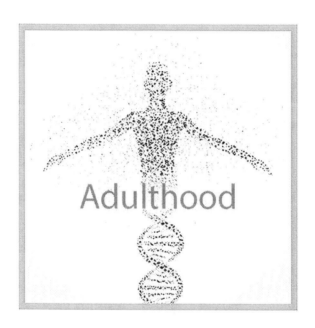

Adulthood

ADULTHOOD

❖ *Conformity is how we have been conditioned to participate in this false sense of security which results in us being out of integrity with ourselves.*

❖ *On a deep, unconscious level we are aware of this and this awareness largely informs our suffering.*

❖ *We abdicate 'the self' by continuing to show up in the world in accordance with the expectations of others which is reinforced by their projections and our reflexive need to defend ourselves in response to those projections.*

❖ *We become imprisoned through fear of what other people will think of us. In an effort to mitigate loss, we participate in the collective conditioning that has us constantly relying on our environment and those who inhabit it to reflect back to us that we exist and are safe, secure, loved and accepted.*

Only the Shadow Knows

The *Shadow Self* is an aspect of the self that is carefully hidden away and personifies everything that we refuse to acknowledge about ourselves. Carl Jung identified it as the *"unknown dark side of the personality which the conscious ego does not identify in itself."* The unconscious rejection of this aspect of the 'self' creates a fundamental 'split' that we are always defending against.

Our social conditioning has taught us that the best way to heal this 'split', and get our emotional needs met, is to rely primarily on those individuals we form relationships with to make us feel better about ourselves. This conditioning is the 'springboard' that propels us into forming co-dependent relationships throughout the course of our lifetime.

The very nature of co-dependency ends up reinforcing the 'wall' or 'façade' that we've created that guards us against acknowledging, embracing and integrating our shadow material. Because we are now completely reliant on the other to make us feel good about ourselves; we can't risk the possibility that they will get a peek beyond the 'wall' that we've created that so carefully guards everything we judge about ourselves.

The belief is that if we allow the 'façade' to drop, then those, whose opinions matter so much to us, will be repulsed. And that is why most of our energies are spent every day ensuring that our shadows will never be exposed to the light of day out of fear of being abandoned by those we love.

One of the central themes in the healing I facilitate for my clients is to acknowledge our *Shadow Self* and to understand that the primary tension that we carry within us at all times is the denial and rejection of this shadow aspect in an unconscious attempt to minimize loss. The key to healing everything is to begin to accept, embrace and integrate all those aspects of ourselves that we despise and loathe and keep carefully hidden away. In order to heal beyond the 'split' towards wholeness and well-being, it is imperative that we plumb these depths. There are no detours.

Our outer world is a continuous reflection of what we believe to be true about ourselves. If we deeply desire to be in a loving relationship with another; then we must first learn how to be in a loving relationship with ourselves. In order to do this, we must first begin to immerse ourselves in those shadow aspects which we've kept carefully hidden from ourselves and others. This is the journey to self-love and self-acceptance; without which, we will never have the capacity to truly love another:

THE SHADOW SELF

" ... For fear threatens the self-image you have so

carefully molded

And it threatens the sexual role you have

chosen

And you dread shame or loss of control

And in relationships you vacillate between

fears of too much closeness or not enough

And you fear the suffering that others can inflict:

criticism and rejection, humiliation and invasion

And vulnerable and insecure, you fear the

aggravation of opening old wounds

And the sense of being overwhelmed by facets

of yourself which have been condemned in the

past, even by yourself as well as others

And your greatest fears may be threats to your

physical body or to your identity

And so you cling to the familiar parental voices

within

Lest you re-experience the traumas of

childhood which could plunge you headlong

into the black abyss of terror; the world of the

frightened, rejected child...abandoned and

alone...

And some inner guardian ardently defends the

gate that seals off the pain and anxiety of old

wounds

When shadows play at the edge of your mind...

Become your shadow-self

Woo the distrustful child out of the darkness

and back to life

For shadows tell us what we fear

And draw smudged pictures of dreads we are

afraid to feel

Penetrate them

Face them and you will balance your inner self

and the persona you present to the outside

world: the mask

For within those smoky depths are stored

nightmares: the worst images we have of

ourselves

Shadows are places of mysterious fears

There is no sun there

And they represent the lowest point; the nadir

of our existence where ghastly forms loom and

lurk in their dark corners, writhing and draping

veils over the light of our days...

For the shadow is the secret arena of the inner

self

And no one outside of ourselves can see it

And when we dare to enter therein, we

disappear

And all of our energies are directed inward

towards the dark unconscious

For its locked-up material must be brought into

the conscious mind if you are ever to feel

complete and whole and at peace

Still, some choose to live in those shadowy

worlds where dreams, nightmares and realities

are forever confused...

Constantly moving in and out of each other

So decisions are impossible to make

And facts are hopelessly distorted by

propaganda or fears

And outward lives reflect the pathetic inner

struggle

As the confused one flits around endlessly in

pointless circles

From task to task

From opinion to empty opinion

And he chatters on, pouring out streams of

words with no substance

Without purpose

Without direction

Without hope

And in encountering your shadow-self, you

may wonder how you can live with the

discovery of your own ugliness and potential

evil

For you will glimpse terrifying energies within,

gaining pleasure from revenge or planning the

downfall of those who have hurt you

And you may even uncover a masochistic

craving for physical or emotional self-abuse

For discovering inner demons is a terrible blow

to your self-esteem

Know that the first experience of bringing those

bad energies out is always the worst

But once out of darkness, they lose power

and evaporate in the light

Learn to trust the beauty within, while

tolerating your darker side

For it is a paradox that the process of spiritual

growth involves lessening your attachment to

your ideal images of self and others and

embracing instead your lowest, most vile self

And if at first you feel threatened or repulsed

by your hidden facets

Know that you can only discover the buried

treasure within by being willing to embrace the

distrustful, uncooperative child

Love and understanding will eventually open

the lock

See the most evil parts of yourself as the

methods of survival for a terrified child whose

needs have been distorted by years of

emotional neglect and abuse

Seek out the child's needs

Meet those needs and soothe his fears

Confront him, touch him

Tell him you are a friend from his future

And that you understand his pain

And you will create for yourself the nurturing

conditions that lead to transformation

Then open the channel of healing love and

compassion for others

For only then will the twisted, unredeemed

facets of yourself and the evil hiding within, be

countered and melted by warm feelings

Then you will at last feel compassion for

Yourself

Zambucka, Kristin. (1999). The Classic Trilogy, Ano 'Ano:
The Seed, The Mana Keepers, The Fire Lily.
Honolulu, Hawaii: Mutual Publishing. Pg. 119-124.

Summary

❖ *The Shadow Self is an aspect of the self that is carefully hidden away and personifies everything that we refuse to acknowledge about ourselves.*

❖ *The unconscious rejection of this aspect of the self creates a fundamental 'split' that we are always defending against.*

❖ *This conditioning is the 'springboard' that propels us into forming co-dependent relationships throughout the course of our lifetime.*

❖ *Our social conditioning has taught us that the best way to heal this 'split', and get our emotional needs met, is to rely primarily on those individuals we form relationships with to make us feel better about ourselves.*

❖ *Most of our energies are spent every day ensuring that our shadows will never be exposed to the light of day out of fear of being abandoned by those we love.*

Defense Mechanisms

Freud described defense mechanisms as the ego's (*personal identity*) unconscious attempt to minimize anxiety in response to conflict occurring between the id (*instinctive impulses*) and the superego (*self-critical conscience*). He identified a core group of eight mechanisms:

Denial: Refusing to accept real events because they are unpleasant. *Example*: Susan won't acknowledge she has substance abuse issues despite not being able to go a day without a drink.

Displacement: Transferring inappropriate behaviors into a venue that evokes less distress. *Example*: Mark is angry at his boss, but does not express it. Instead, he waits until he gets home and vents his anger onto his wife and children.

Projection: Attributing what is perceived as unacceptable desires and behaviors onto others. *Example*: Barbara accuses her husband of cheating on her because she has been cheating on him for years.

Rationalization: Creating false excuses for one's perceived failures or unacceptable behaviors. *Example:* George justifies cheating on the exam by identifying that everyone else cheated.

Reaction Formation: Perceiving one's true feelings to be socially unacceptable, so acts in opposition to those feelings in what is usually an exaggerated performance. *Example:* Kim 'hero-worships' her father, despite him being physically abusive towards her.

Regression: Relying on coping mechanisms from a less mature stage of development. *Example:* After 10 year old Sally's newborn brother came home, she began to suck her thumb.

Repression: Suppressing painful memories and thoughts. *Example:* Patrick is unable to remember the details of how his father drowned despite being present when it happened.

Sublimation: Redirecting socially unacceptable desires into more acceptable channels. *Example:* Richard's anger towards the drunk driver who killed his brother is taken out on his opponents when he plays football.

Beyond the construct of id, ego and superego; I describe defense mechanisms as emotional reflexes that become activated when the individual is 'triggered' by a stimulus in the environment that has touched on an anxiety-provoking memory.

The 'trigger' occurs as a result of whatever is happening being in resonance with a cellular memory of a moment in time that would have been threatening and overwhelming to the physical and emotional body. As a result, the adrenals become activated and the nervous system becomes dysregulated, resulting in the defense mechanisms becoming activated in an attempt to minimize the anxiety response.

Without realizing it, we have all unconsciously developed an array of well-honed defense mechanisms over the years to help us navigate and cope with uncomfortable and anxiety-provoking situations. The following is my list of defense mechanisms that are present every day in the sessions I facilitate for my clients. They include, but are not limited to:

Idealizing or **devaluing** others through comparison in order to regulate one's own self-esteem.

Altruism allows for vicariously gratifying experiences which include fulfilling the needs of others to the detriment of the self.

Humor expresses feelings overtly without having to experience personal discomfort. Sarcasm is a common expression of this defense mechanism and is used to distance oneself from one's own anger.

Passive aggressive expressions of anger towards others through passivity and turning against the self through failure, procrastination, resentment, victimology and martyrdom.

Controlling people and events in order to minimize anxiety.

Intellectualization focuses primarily on external reality in order to avoid intimacy with self and others through expressions of feelings.

What is most important to understand is that when we are expressing through these defense mechanisms we are attempting to get our physical and emotional needs met in an extremely distorted and unhealthy manner that is a direct reflection of our own distorted self-image. This distorted self-image creates an internal conflict which has us in a chronic state of tension. By relying on these unconscious defense mechanisms to deflect what it is we are unable to accept about ourselves, and alleviate the anxiety associated with this inner tension; we have only managed to minimize our discomfort until the next uncomfortable situation arises.

Consequently, these defense mechanisms continue to inform dysfunctional behavioral and relationship patterns that reinforce our distorted self-image and become the stumbling blocks that prevent us from experiencing the quality of life we truly desire. Therapy provides an opportunity to increase our awareness around what it is that is preventing us from having our preferred experience by identifying what our defense mechanisms are so that we can begin to eliminate them.

The key to eliminating them is to engage in a process of learning how to love and accept ourselves. In doing so, we integrate those aspects of ourselves that we have rejected; that we hide from others out of fear and shame. By integrating our wounded aspects, we heal our distorted self-image and from this place of wholeness and authenticity; there is no longer the need to defend ourselves.

Summary

❖ *Defense mechanisms are emotional reflexes that become activated when the individual is 'triggered' by a stimulus in the environment that has touched on an anxiety-provoking memory.*

❖ *The 'trigger' occurs in response to the stimulus being in resonance with a cellular memory of a moment in time that would have been threatening and overwhelming to the physical and emotional body.*

❖ *The adrenals become activated and the nervous system becomes dysregulated, resulting in the defense mechanisms becoming activated in an attempt to minimize the anxiety response.*

❖ *We have all unconsciously developed an array of well-honed defense mechanisms over the years to help us navigate and cope with uncomfortable and anxiety-provoking situations.*

The Dance of Relationship

On the back of my business card can be found the following quote from the Buddhist monk, Thich Nhat Hanh:

"You must love in such a way
that the person you love feels free."

It is my belief that if we are practicing anything other than this sentiment; we are not participating in a loving relationship with our self or others. To go one step further, I've come to believe that most of what is identified by our cultural and social conditioning as expressions of love between two individuals is not at all, but rather, conditional, need-based expressions of extreme co-dependency. Terms like 'soul-mate' and 'better-half' along with expressions such as *"you complete me"*, *"I owe my happiness to you"*, *"you are my whole world"*, *"you make me feel special"*, and *"till death do us part"* not only fuel the billion dollar greeting card , romance novel and 'made-for-tv' movie industries; but also reinforce fear-based imprinting that sets us up to continuously recreate and participate in these dysfunctional relationships. This dawning awareness has been extremely significant for my own personal healing and growth as well as for the work I facilitate for my clients.

I believe that all relationships are sacred workshops. The extent to which we experience them as such is determined by our level of self-awareness. The reason I refer to them as workshops is because there is always an opportunity for us to move beyond our own imprinting and subsequent patterns by working consciously with the material that comes up in response to dancing in relationship with another. Much of the time I spend with clients is focused on assisting them with this specific understanding. Until we are willing to engage in such an inquiry, we will always be dancing with, what I like to describe as, 'eyes wide shut'. This lack of awareness sets us up to continuously cycle through dysfunctional relationship patterns that leave us feeling unfulfilled and rejected because we believe that, over time, the person we fell in love with was unable to fulfill our needs and, therefore, did not love us as much as we initially thought or as much as we believe we loved them.

So the dance that I'm referring to in *The Dance of Relationship* is an energetic dance that has largely been influenced by what we are not aware of. What we choose to focus on and the stories we create about our experience while in relationship with the other, rarely, if ever, describes what is actually occurring. This is why, in my humble opinion, most 'couple's counseling' venues are extremely ineffective in achieving any significant changes within the underlying patterns and dynamics of the relationship.

I would also go so far as to say that if the focus is primarily on the narrative of each participant; then the dysfunctional patterns that are pervasive in the relationship will actually end up being reinforced. It's important to remember that the stories we create around our experiences are part of our well-honed defense mechanisms that ensure that we deflect and distance ourselves from connecting to what it is we don't want to feel in reference to our experiences and subsequent wound imprinting.

Referring to the description of what a wound imprint is from the **BTI** modality:

"Prenatal, perinatal and childhood experiences which should include appropriate environmental stimulus and responsiveness to our needs, not only prevents distress, but also ensures that the limbic brain which receives and processes sensations, feelings and emotions 'imprints' these experiences as cellular memory in the body, validating our right to exist."

"If these experiences are less nurturing and more painful, our limbic system begins to 'imprint' these experiences on the cellular level as distorted expressions of love."

During childhood and adolescence:

"Our schemas develop around this conditioning, which informs all of our beliefs and perceptions about our self, others, and our environment; including the unconscious need to control or be controlled in order to feel safe and secure."

"This sets us up to recreate these experiences in a cyclical fashion throughout life; informing chronic dysfunctional relationship patterns in an unconscious attempt to get our physical and emotional needs met."

The degree to which the individual has been traumatized and 'shattered' during their most critical stages of development will always determine their capacity to be truly vulnerable and intimate while in relationship with self and others.

By the time we reach adulthood:

"We have become imprisoned through fear of what other people will think of us. In an effort to mitigate loss, we participate in the collective conditioning that has us constantly relying on our environment and those who inhabit it (including our closest relationships) to reflect back to us that we exist and are safe, secure, loved and accepted."

While participating in the *Dance of Relationship*:

"We are conditioned to look outside of ourselves in order to identify who and what is causing us pain or pleasure."

Because of this conditioning:

"We will always be trying to manipulate and control our environment and those in it in an attempt to mitigate loss and minimize our suffering."

This ensures that we will:

"Continue to show up in the world in accordance with the expectations of others which is reinforced by their projections onto us and our reflexive need to defend ourselves in response to those projections."

In short, as long as we rely on those who we are in relationship with to make us feel better about ourselves; we will continue to participate in co-dependent relationships. Since we come together in relationship at the level of our respective wounding; our capacity to truly love one another will always be limited by this dynamic.

"In order to move beyond our unconscious reliance on our environment to reassure us that we are safe and secure; we must begin to dissolve our wound imprinting."

"Our journey towards integration and wholeness requires that our attention be directed primarily inward to resolve whatever trauma imprinting and subsequent self-judgments we are defending against that reinforce our beliefs that we are not enough".

Only then will we be able to move beyond the 'dance' of co-dependency towards self-love, self-acceptance and unconditional love for self and others. Only then will we, and those we love, be free.

Summary

❖ *Most of what is identified by our cultural and social conditioning as expressions of love between two individuals is actually conditional, need-based, expressions of extreme co-dependency.*

❖ *Fear-based, cellular/wound imprinting sets us up to continuously recreate and participate in these dysfunctional relationships.*

❖ *There is always an opportunity for us to move beyond our imprinting and subsequent patterns by working consciously with the material that comes up in response to 'dancing' in relationship with another.*

❖ *The stories we create around our experiences are part of our well-honed defense mechanisms that ensure that we deflect and distance ourselves from connecting to what it is we don't want to feel in reference to our experiences and subsequent wound imprinting.*

❖ *If the focus is primarily on the narrative of each participant; the dysfunctional patterns that are pervasive in the relationship will actually end up being reinforced.*

❖ *The extent to which the individual has been traumatized during their most critical stages of development will always limit their capacity to be truly vulnerable and intimate while in relationship.*

Patterns

Our identities are deeply woven within the stories we tell about ourselves, our relationships and our experiences. These stories not only reflect our distorted self-image, but also our distorted perceptions of others. For this reason it is imperative that the therapeutic focus never be on the client's narrative.

When the focus remains on the client's narrative, dysfunctional behavioral and relationship patterns become reinforced within the victim/perpetrator framework in which the client always presents as the victim. These patterns are reinforced because the imprinting which was encoded at the cellular level at a much earlier time in their development is reinforced by allowing the client to cycle through stories of having been deceived, betrayed and victimized in the present.

Rather than accommodate countless sessions of having the client cycle through these stories; *BTI Therapy* makes the important distinction between what was imprinted at a much earlier stage of development and what is showing up in their current relationships and environment that is in resonance with these imprints.

This distinction is a much more neutral approach to helping the client conceptualize their experience.

Once again, trauma imprinting occurs when the individual experiences something that is so overwhelming and threatening that the memory becomes *'flash-frozen'* in the frequency of fear at the cellular/molecular level. This makes the individual vulnerable to cycle through endless patterns of similar experiences throughout the course of their lifetime. This pattern is always playing out at the unconscious, cellular level.

The distinction between what's occurring in the present as a reflection of what has already occurred in the past allows the client to understand that their emotional reactivity to what's occurring in the moment is coming from unresolved memory held in the body from earlier traumatic experiences.

This distinction also allows the client the opportunity to create 'space' between what is occurring in the moment and their response to what is occurring. By doing so, they can now begin to shift cyclical patterns of dysfunctional behavior that have unconsciously informed the dynamics underlying all of their personal and professional relationships.

Patterns are the one consistent thread that weaves through everyone's life experience. Learning how to identify and track patterns allows a well-trained clinician to predict the future with tremendous accuracy. Teaching the client how to do this is the greatest gift the clinician has to offer to someone choosing to move beyond their own debilitating and dysfunctional behavioral/relationship patterns.

Patterns consistently reflect the dysfunctional manner in which we show up in the world on a daily basis in an attempt to get our emotional and physical needs met. So it is never helpful to support the client's belief that what is happening in the moment is being determined by someone else and is the reason why they are unable to actualize their desired experience. By focusing on the client's narrative, the therapist is perpetuating the distorted perception that the client's ability to have a different experience is dependent on their alcoholic spouse getting sober or their sociopathic boss developing empathic abilities.

By focusing primarily on the client's behavioral and relationship patterns, the focus shifts from the client's external landscape to their internal landscape; requiring them to take control and ownership of their experience in order to change it. As long as the client is allowed to focus on their narrative which is always about what the other person is doing wrong; then they will continue to replicate their unwelcome experiences in the form of dysfunctional patterns. The names and the locations might change in their story, but the patterns will always persist.

Since our patterns are specific to, and reflections of, our own wound imprinting at the cellular level; the primary focus within the therapeutic venue should always be directed towards the self rather than the stories we tell about the other.

The good news is that once you are able to take ownership for what you have created in your life with *'eyes wide shut'* then you will begin to realize that it is just as possible to create something completely different for yourself 'eyes *wide open'*; something that is much more aligned with expressions of mental, emotional and physical well-being and balance.

Summary

❖ *Our identities are deeply woven within the stories we tell about ourselves, our relationships and our experiences.*

❖ *These stories not only reflect our distorted perceptions of others, but also our own self-image. For this reason it is imperative that the therapeutic focus never be on the client's narrative.*

❖ *When the focus stays on the client's narrative, dysfunctional behavioral and relationship patterns end up being reinforced within the victim/ perpetrator framework in which the client always presents as the victim.*

❖ *These patterns are then reinforced because the imprinting which was encoded at the cellular level at a much earlier time in their development is reinforced by allowing the client to cycle through stories of having been deceived, betrayed and victimized in the present.*

❖ *Since our patterns are specific to, and reflections of, our own wound imprinting at the cellular level; the primary focus within the therapeutic venue should always be directed towards the self rather than the stories we tell about the other.*

❖ *Our patterns consistently reflect the dysfunctional manner in which we show up in the world on a daily basis in an attempt to get our emotional and physical needs met.*

❖ *By focusing primarily on the client's behavioral and relationship patterns, the client is required to take control and ownership of their experience in order to change it.*

Poverty and Violence

"People say walking on water is a miracle, but to me walking peacefully on earth is the real miracle."

- Thich Nhat Hanh -

Mahatma Gandhi once said that poverty was the worst form of violence. I agree with his sentiment, but would change it slightly to say that poverty is the most insidious form of violence. The reason I think this distinction is important is because it addresses the understanding that poverty is a firmly established demographic within the socioeconomic fabric of a country that is rarely apparent to individuals who are not struggling to meet their basic needs on a daily basis. As soon as we are able to accept that identification, it brings a heightened level of awareness and concern to a subject that we, as a collective, have otherwise become extremely complacent to by accepting that it has been, and will always be, a part of the demographics that make up any society, including one as affluent as the United States.

Pope Francis expounded on this social injustice during a trip to the U.S. when he acknowledged the divide between some of the world's wealthiest and *"those considered disposable because they are only considered as part of a statistic."* While speaking in New York City to the *United Nation's General Assembly* he urged them to work together to push a global agenda of peace and identified that *"big cities conceal the faces of all those people who don't appear to belong, or are second-class citizens."* During a stop in Washington D.C., he demonstrated his compassion for these 'second-class citizens' by choosing to have lunch with the homeless rather than members of congress.

As long as poverty exists, equality is impossible to achieve. Without equality, we will always have a very small percentage of the population able to access political powers through huge monetary donations in an effort to influence legislation and social policies that ensure that they will always be able to maintain their scope of power, money and influence at the expense of the most vulnerable populations.

Between the end of World War II and the late 1970s, incomes in the United States were becoming more equal. Incomes at the bottom were rising faster than those at the top. However, since the late 1970s, this trend has reversed. Between 1979 and 2012, the top 5 percent of American families saw their real incomes increase 74.9 percent while the lowest 5 percent saw a decrease in real income of 12.1 percent. This increasing disparity ensures that political access is concentrated at the top, resulting in a small group of individuals who are in control and unresponsive to the needs of ordinary people. Pope Francis's position is that you would have to be less than human to not be concerned by this contrast and imbalance. Gandhi believed that this contrast was an expression of contempt, indifference and violence, and that these individuals who continue to inflict poverty through this well-honed and widely accepted political power-dynamic are the worst criminals in history.

Despite being the wealthiest nation in the world, the United States has the highest levels of poverty than any other western democracy. In 2012, 46.5 million people, comprised of 16.1 million children, were living in poverty. These statistics are more on par with Romania than with countries like Canada, France or Germany, making it extremely difficult to accept that this country is actually a true democracy.

On a much smaller, yet equally troubling scale, I happen to live in a small university town that was once home to Thomas Jefferson. It is a mecca for intellectual, artistic, culinary, entrepreneurial and musical pursuits. At first glance, it appears to be made up primarily of extremely comfortable and affluent populations. However, a recent report released by the *Charlottesville Works Initiative* identified that in a city of 45,538 residents, over 27% of the population lives below the poverty line. That translates to 12,295 men, women and children who lack self-sufficiency because they are struggling every day to meet their basic needs.

In 2014, *Feeding America* found that Charlottesville had a food insecurity rate of 17.9% overall and 14.8% for children; which means that 8,151 individuals, comprised of 6,740 children, do not know where their next meal is coming from. A 2014 study by the *University of Virginia* identified that poverty and its consequences; such as inadequate nutrition, persistent anxiety and intellectual/emotional impairments, affect the daily lives of 615,479 children living in the state of Virginia.

During the first five years of my post-graduate work, I worked exclusively with these at-risk populations and got to see up close the long-term, multi-generational impact that economic distress and poverty inflicts on individuals and families. It is an environment of uncertainty in which the most fundamental and basic necessities of life, such as food and shelter, are not guaranteed; and the legacy of such extreme uncertainty, at the basic level of survival, continues well beyond childhood.

Neuroimaging studies have shown that poverty is closely associated with smaller brain volumes in areas involved in emotional processing as well as impaired cognitive functioning in areas of language, memory and executive functioning tasks. In addition, prolonged stress associated with extreme poverty increases the risk of mood disorders such as depression, anxiety and post-traumatic stress disorder; leading to job loss and social isolation.

Abraham Maslow was a psychologist who identified in his 1943 paper "*A Theory of Human Motivation*" that people are motivated to achieve certain needs and identified those needs in a 5-stage hierarchical model shaped like a pyramid. Beginning at the bottom of the model, the five stages are physiological, safety, love/belonging, esteem and actualization. The two lowest tiers encompass basic physical needs such as food and shelter, including the need to feel safe and secure. According to this theory, every person has the desire to move up the hierarchy toward the level of self-actualization. Unfortunately, progress will always be disrupted by an inability to meet the most basic needs.

In my private practice, the primary focus is in helping the individual move towards greater expressions of self-actualization. Much of the time is spent identifying, challenging and healing whatever 'imprints' are informing beliefs and perceptions that limit the individual's capacity to move beyond the four lower tiers in *Maslow's Hierarchy of Needs*. However, whatever level the individual is functioning at, is what determines where we begin the therapeutic process. Career counseling, child care, transportation, health and nutrition are all topics that end up being explored in an effort to move the individual beyond the level of 'survival'. Only then does it make sense to explore topics such as self-esteem, integrity, creativity, spontaneity and spirituality. Regardless of where we begin, the fundamental understanding is that the individual has the capacity to take this journey but must first 'unhook' from the perception that external forces will always control and determine their experience. This is a BIG part of the social, economic and cultural conditioning that we've been at the effect of for thousands of years. Maslow believed that only one in a hundred people become fully self-actualized because our society rewards extrinsic motivation based on esteem, acceptance and love.

Intrinsic motivation refers to a quality of motivation that comes from within the individual rather than from any external reward. Performing a task or action for the sake of pure pleasure and enjoyment is an example of intrinsic motivation. Identifying what *'feeds the soul'* and *'nourishes the heart',* and acting on it, is the key to moving to the top tier of Maslow's pyramid. However, when you're extrinsically motivated to do something, you're not concerned with whether or not the action is enjoyable, but whether or not the outcomes will meet your basic physical and emotional needs.

If an individual has experienced a childhood full of chronic stress and trauma associated with extreme poverty; the biggest impediment in moving beyond that experience is social conditioning. Seeking and realizing personal potential and growth is everyone's birthright. Imagine if we lived in a country that was not violent; a country in which the distribution of wealth was more balanced and every man, woman and child lived in the safety and security of having a roof over their heads while knowing where their next meal was coming from. Imagine how that would impact everyone. Imagine a life that was not fueled by fear and anxiety. Imagine a life in which intellectual, creative and spiritual pursuits were the primary focus; in which our social conditioning confirmed that personal freedom was the expected outcome.

Imagine that.

Summary

❖ As of 2012, poverty and economic distress impacted as many as 46.5 million children and families in the United States.

❖ Neuroimaging studies have shown that poverty is closely associated with smaller brain volumes in areas involved in emotional processing, and impaired cognitive functioning in areas of language, memory and executive functioning tasks.

❖ Prolonged stress associated with extreme poverty increases the risk of mood disorders such as depression, anxiety and post-traumatic stress disorder; leading to job loss and social isolation.

❖ Seeking and realizing personal potential and growth is everyone's birthright but can only be achieved in a country where the distribution of wealth is more balanced and every man, woman, and child is living in the safety and security of having a roof over their heads while knowing where their next meal is coming from.

Adrenal Fatigue

Prior to writing this book, I understood what adrenal fatigue was relative to my own experience and those of my clients. After doing some additional research for this book; it turns out, ironically, that I still had much to learn, including the fact that I met the criteria for *Adrenal Fatigue*. This is such a wonderful reminder that we are always teaching what it is we most need to learn. So let's begin to learn about this subject together by finding out what adrenals are, where they are located and what function they serve.

Adrenals are two triangular-shaped glands that sit on top of the kidneys and are approximately 1.5 inches wide and 3 inches long. They are made up of two parts; the *adrenal cortex* and the *adrenal medulla*. The *adrenal cortex* is the outer part of the gland and produces hormones that are vital to life such as *cortisol* which helps regulate metabolism and helps the body respond to stress, and *aldosterone* which helps regulate the blood pressure. The *adrenal medulla* is the inner part of the gland and produces *adrenaline*; also known as *epinephrine*, which is the hormone that helps the body spring into action in response to stressful situations by increasing heart rate, rushing blood to muscles and the brain, and spiking blood sugar by helping convert *glycogen* to *glucose* in the liver. *Norepinephrine*, also known as *noradrenaline*, works with *epinephrine* in responding to stress; causing the narrowing of blood vessels which can, over time, result in high blood pressure.

Corticosteroid hormones balance stress response, energy flow, body temperature, water balance and other essential processes. The *adrenal cortex* produces two main groups of them; the *glucocorticoids* and the *mineralocorticoids,* which chemically control some of the most basic actions necessary to protect, nourish and maintain the body.

Glucocorticoids include *hydrocortisone,* commonly known as *cortisol,* which regulates how the body converts fats, proteins and carbohydrates to energy, and helps regulate blood pressure and cardiovascular function. It also includes *corticosterone,* which is the hormone that works with *hydrocortisone* to regulate immune response, and suppress inflammatory reactions.

If stress is causing your *cortisol* levels to be elevated, this anti-inflammatory response becomes too strong. This effectively stops your immune system from working properly and this weakened state can last as long as whatever is causing the stress. Without a properly functioning immune system, you become vulnerable to disease. When the adrenals become fatigued; they struggle to release the necessary amount of hormones, causing the immune system to over-react to pathogens, resulting in chronic inflammation, auto-immune diseases and decreased strength, focus and awareness.

As you can see, the adrenal glands play a large role within the endocrine system by regulating and maintaining many of our vital internal processes. *Adrenal Fatigue* is now being referred to as the *Syndrome of the 21st Century* by many holistic physicians and therapists despite the fact that the scientific community refuses to acknowledge its existence.

This is interesting when you consider that it is now widely recognized, even within the scientific community, that most, if not all, chronic disease expressions have inflammation as an underlying antecedent, which is a hallmark symptom of *adrenal fatigue*.

The following is a list of symptoms which are strong indicators that your adrenals may be fatigued:

- *Difficulty falling asleep*
- *Difficulty waking up*
- *Easily stressed*
- *Headaches*
- *Weight gain*
- *Auto-immune issues*
- *Low thyroid functioning*
- *High blood pressure*

- *Low blood sugar*
- *Feelings of apathy, irritability and anxiety*
- *Muscle and joint pain*
- *Digestive issues*
- *Inability to relax*
- *Inability to maintain mental focus*
- *Inability to recover appropriately from exercise*

Stress is a specific response by the body to a stimulus, such as fear or pain, which disturbs or interferes with normal physiological equilibrium. It can be physical, mental, emotional, chronic or acute. We now live in a very busy world in which we are exposed to 24-hour mainstream and social media coverage of violent, stressful, painful and fearful stimuli. In addition, lifestyle stressors such as lack of sleep, poor diet, use of stimulants, striving for perfectionism, 'pushing through' a project or a day despite being tired, staying in unhappy relationships, and working every day in a stressful environment, all contribute to impaired adrenal function. Our physical bodies are just not 'hard-wired' to withstand such chronic stress and still be able to maintain physical and emotional equilibrium despite social conditioning that tells us every day that our value and worth increases with how much we do. The concept of just 'being' is extremely counter-intuitive and de-valued in our society.

Effective treatment for *Adrenal Fatigue* includes a combination of a healthy diet, minerals, vitamins, amino acids, herbal support, exercise and proper sleep.

In reference to the supplements listed below, manual muscle testing is strongly recommended to determine the appropriate dosage for each individual:

* *Organic, high quality proteins*
* *Organic vegetables and fruit*
* *Omega 3 fatty acids manage inflammation and minimize the loop that feeds into higher cortisol production*
* *Mineral sea salt added to food and water*
* *Vitamin C mitigates high cortisol response while inducing an anti-inflammatory response*
* *Vitamin B Complex; all B vitamins are critical for the entire adrenal cascade while Vitamin B5 is especially important in helping to restore the adrenal glands*
* *Magnesium is essential to the production of the enzymes and energy necessary for the adrenal cascade*
* *Liquid adrenal support by Herb Pharm strengthens and restores the adrenals and includes Eleuthero Root, Licorice Root, Sarsaparilla Root, Oat Milky Seed, and Prickly Ash Bark*
* *Free Form Amino Acid Complex provides all of the necessary 'building blocks' for the production of body proteins, has a broad application for both mental and physical functions, supports hormone, enzyme and antibody formation, supports healthy nervous system function*
* *DHEA (Dehydroepiandrosterone) is a hormone that comes from the adrenal gland as well as the brain*

and is responsible for the production of androgens and estrogens; it begins to decrease after the age of 30; evidence suggests that DHEA may help treat depression, obesity and osteoporosis

❖ *L-Theanine is a calming amino acid that works by increasing GABA which increases a sense of well-being*

❖ *L-5-HTP is a naturally occurring amino acid that converts to Serotonin and Melatonin*

In addition to making dietary and supplemental changes, lifestyle changes are usually required to re-balance the brain and the body long-term. This is a subject that is often explored in many of my therapy sessions with clients. If one truly desires to enhance their over-all sense of well-being; then every arena in one's life needs to be excavated and explored. Toxic and stressful relationships, including one's work environment, are just as debilitating to the mind and body as a poor diet. A lack of self-care and a tendency to overextend ourselves is a reflection of how little we value ourselves and is always being informed by our imprinting and conditioning. The road to recovery from all things physical, mental and emotional requires a re-orientation on the subject of self-care. Learning that self-care is nothing more than an expression of self-love, is a critical part of everyone's healing journey.

Summary

❖ *Adrenal glands play a large role within the endocrine system by regulating and maintaining many of our vital internal processes.*

❖ *When the adrenals become fatigued, they struggle to release the necessary amount of hormones causing the immune system to over-react to pathogens, resulting in chronic inflammation, auto-immune diseases and decreased strength, focus and awareness.*

❖ *Most chronic diseases have inflammation as an underlying antecedent which is a hallmark symptom of Adrenal Fatigue.*

❖ *Stress is a specific response by the body to stimulus such as fear, pain or exhaustion that interferes with normal physiological equilibrium.*

❖ *Our physical bodies are not able to withstand chronic stress, and still be able to maintain normal equilibrium, despite social conditioning that tells us every day that our value and worth increases with how much we do.*

❖ *Effective treatment for Adrenal Fatigue includes a combination of a healthy diet, minerals, vitamins, amino acids, herbal support, exercise and proper sleep.*

Substance Abuse

I believe that a large part of my effectiveness as an 'agent-of-change' when working with my clients, directly relates to whether or not I've actually experienced and navigated the same challenges they are attempting to recover from and move beyond. As it relates to substance abuse, this correlation is especially true.

I began drinking alcohol at the age of eight. By the time I was twelve I was frequently impaired. The first time I drove a car at the age of fifteen was the first time I 'dropped' acid. For a period of ten years between the ages of fifteen and twenty-five, I was stoned on something every single day. Alcohol, marijuana, hashish and magic mushrooms were the most common substances of choice on a daily basis. Cocaine and LSD were usually reserved for special occasions such as birthdays, graduations and weddings.

Despite my extended proclivity for not being fully present in my mind, body or this dimension; I somehow managed to complete high school in three years and graduate from University by the age of twenty-four.

The good news is; I survived these years of extended impairment despite there being no rational explanation as to why I'm still alive. The sad news is; my brain and body were significantly compromised due to engaging in extreme, at-risk behaviors while under the influence of one or more mind-altering substances. Lots of broken bones, severe concussions, and a small neurological event; referred to as a mild stroke, at the age of eighteen, ensured that I will never truly know the full capacity of the mental or physical acuity I came into this world with.

However, an important part of my recovery was to learn and understand what all of the factors and influences were, both psychological and physiological, that put me at incredible risk for such an extended period of time during my most formative years. Many of these insights are now embodied within my clinical practice as well as the modality that this book is based upon.

Two of those insights are as follows:

1) I inherited a strong, genetic predisposition to addiction through the DNA of my maternal and paternal lineages; the O'Connell's and the McGowan's.

2) I was extremely vulnerable to manifest addiction as a disease expression and a coping mechanism in response to significant chronic stress and trauma I experienced throughout childhood and adolescence.

At the end of my first year of graduate school, in the summer of 2004, I was provided the opportunity to return to the substance abuse recovery center that I had attended as an outpatient in 1995 in order to complete my graduate internship requirement. This proved to be and incredibly surreal and satisfying experience for having come full-circle in the space of nine years.

Having sat on both sides of the room as both client and clinician, I bring a much wider perspective to the issue of recovery from substance abuse and life in general; one that is far more holistic and non-judgmental. And because the recovery framework I participated in was scientifically and biochemically based, lasting change actually occurred beyond the endless cycles of relapse that more than often characterize this complex and challenging issue.

Understanding Addiction through the Biochemical Paradigm

The Baldwin Research Institute is a not-for-profit corporation approved by the New York State Department of Education as an institute conducting alcohol and drug research. Baldwin Research began its efforts in 1989 when it conducted studies of modern Alcoholics Anonymous and Narcotics Anonymous and their claims of success rates as high as 93 percent. Baldwin Research was unable to validate a single treatment program with a success rate greater than 3 percent. Despite there being no research to date to support the efficacy of the 12-step model of recovery;

90% of addiction treatment facilities in the United States employ this approach.

This is one reason why adequate treatment continues to elude the current medical model. Many people still believe that 12-step interactive group psychotherapy can help individuals abusing drugs and alcohol achieve sobriety through self-understanding. This perception diverts attention from the physical causes of alcohol and drug abuse and can compound the individual's guilt and shame by encouraging them to surrender to a *higher power*, pray to have their *defects of character* lifted, and to accept their *powerlessness*.

The concept of addiction being a moral failure is still evidenced by our country's investment in criminal justice rather than treatment. It is estimated that as many as 165,000 people are court-mandated to attend AA and NA meetings annually in the United States. Consequently, the need for community education is as strong as ever.

During the past thirty years, biochemical research has created a new paradigm of understanding that invites us to treat substance abuse problems more effectively at the cellular and molecular level. This has allowed the field of psychiatry to change its thinking about addiction disorders; moving them from categories of moral failures to brain diseases.

Millions of chemical reactions occur every second in the trillions of cells that make up our bodies.

Biochemical imbalance can result from inadequate nutrients being supplied to these cells. These nutrients are the raw materials that allow our cells to carry out these complex chemical reactions. If left uncorrected, biochemical imbalance can result in physical and mental deterioration.

Imbalances in the biochemistry of brain cells, known as neurons, can affect our moods and our behavior dramatically. Biochemical explanations focus on neurotransmitters as playing a key role in the cycle of dependency as manifested in the brain disease of addiction. Neurotransmitters are chemicals in the brain, which act as messengers between the neurons, controlling every aspect of our behaviors.

Feelings of optimal well-being are radically compromised when the brain's ability to produce adequate supplies of these neurotransmitters is suppressed through the chronic use of alcohol and other potentially addictive substances. When neurotransmitter availability is reduced, too few receptor sites are filled, resulting in symptoms that include craving, depression and anxiety. To ease these symptoms, the use of alcohol or drugs is repeated. The cycle continues, resulting in increased tolerance and the need for more frequent use. Chronic intoxication can cause behavioral changes and irreversible brain damage, disabling the person for a lifetime.

Treatment is often difficult because of such poor recovery rates and the social stigma attached to the condition. However, it is important for the alcoholic or addict to understand that the symptoms of their disease, such as cravings and withdrawal are not character flaws. Therefore, they should expect the same level of care, concern and compassion that anyone diagnosed with a chronic and potentially fatal disease would expect to receive.

The nutritional components of a treatment program take on tremendous significance for long-term, successful recovery since neurotransmitters are made up of amino acids and certain vitamins and minerals influence the conversion of amino acids into neurotransmitters. For example, vitamin C is involved in the conversion of *dopamine* to *norepinephrine*; vitamin B6 is involved in the conversion of *phenylalanine* to *dopamine* and *tryptophan* to *serotonin,* while zinc influences the metabolism of neurotransmitters in general.

The following chart outlines the amino acid deficiency symptoms and the corresponding amino acids necessary to supplement the brain, depending on the individual's drug(s) of choice:

Amino Acid	Restored Brain Chemical	Addictive Substance	Amino Acid Deficiency Symptoms	Behavioral Change
D-Phenylalanine or DL-Phenylalanine	Enkephalins Endorphins	Heroin, Alcohol Marijuana Sweets, Starches Tobacco	Sensitive to pain Cravings for food, drugs, comfort, and pleasure	Anti-craving Anti-depression Increased energy, focus & pleasure.
L-Tyrosine	Norepinephrine Dopamine	Caffeine, Speed Cocaine, Marijuana Alcohol, Tobacco Sweets, Starches	Depression Low energy Cravings Inability to focus	Anti-craving Anti-depression Increased energy, focus & pleasure.
L-Tryptophan 5-HTP	Serotonin	Alcohol Marijuana Ecstasy Tobacco Starches Sweets	Irritability Cravings Insomnia Anxiety Depression	Improved mood Anti-craving Anti-depression Anti-anxiety Anti-insomnia
GABA	GABA	Valium, Alcohol Marijuana Tobacco Sweets, Starches	Stressed Nervous Tense Muscles Difficulty Relaxing	Calm Relaxed
L-Glutamine	Fuel Source for Entire Brain	Alcohol Sweets Starches	Stressed Mood Swings Hypoglycemia	Relaxed Moods stabilized Blood Sugar stabilized

Amino acids are critical for stopping cravings because they are the essential building blocks of the neurotransmitters that tell the brain whether or not we are satisfied. As a result, nutrition plays a critical role in healing alcoholism and addiction because key nutrients can help restore the pre-existing neurotransmitter deficiencies which helps heal the body from the destructive physiological effects caused by this addiction.

The frontal lobe region in our brains is the primary location of the neurotransmitter activity associated with alcohol and drug abuse. This area, located behind the forehead, is thought by neurobiologists to be one of the last areas of the brain to develop. It also accounts for characteristics considered uniquely human, such as artistic expression, subtle humor, creative thinking and the ability to project what the probable consequences of our actions might be. It is not until we reach our mid-20's that our frontal lobes are completely developed.

For this reason, it is imperative that we develop educational tools and information for young people based on the biochemical understanding of alcohol and drug addiction. Alcohol and drug use disrupts the development and growth of the very parts of our brain that separate us from other mammals.

Historically, relapse prevention has focused on cognitive and behavioral modification techniques to counteract biological cravings and the conditioning process associated with chronic addiction. However, Abraham Maslow aptly demonstrated that an individual's foundation for building towards self-actualization must be physical stabilization. This stabilization process in substance abuse and addiction must involve the improvement of brain chemistry capabilities. Nutritional supplement combinations are available that dramatically enhance neurotransmitter availability and hasten the individual's recovery towards long-term, higher level functioning manifesting in acceptable behaviors, increased confidence as well as positive feelings and thoughts.

Summary

❖ *Within the past thirty years, biochemical research has created a new paradigm of understanding that invites us to treat substance abuse problems more effectively at the cellular and molecular level.*

❖ *The biochemical framework for addiction recovery focuses on neurotransmitters which play a critical role in the cycle of drug and alcohol dependency.*

❖ *Neurotransmitters are chemicals in the brain, which act as messengers between the neurons and essentially control every aspect of our behavior.*

❖ *Feelings of optimal well-being are radically compromised when the brain's ability to produce adequate supplies of these neurotransmitters is suppressed through the chronic use of alcohol and other potentially addictive substances.*

❖ When neurotransmitter availability is reduced, too few receptor sites are filled, resulting in symptoms that include craving, depression and anxiety.

❖ To ease these symptoms, the use of alcohol or drugs is repeated. The endless cycle of abuse continues, resulting in increased tolerance and a need for more frequent drug use.

❖ Amino acids are critical for stopping cravings because they are the essential building blocks of the neurotransmitters that tell the brain whether or not we are satisfied.

❖ Nutrition plays a critical role in healing alcoholism and addiction because key nutrients can help restore pre-existing neurotransmitter deficiencies and help heal the body from the destructive physiological effects caused by this addiction.

The DSM, the APA, and Big Pharma

The Diagnostic Statistical Manual (DSM) is considered the bible of American psychiatry. It provides diagnostic criteria to assist qualified clinicians in making mental disorder diagnoses in order to treat clients whose symptoms and behaviors meet the criteria for those disorders.

The American Psychiatric Association (APA) published its first diagnostic manuals in 1952 and 1968 which were spiral bound booklets comprised of 130 pages. In 1980 the *DSM-III* was a 494 page hardbound book and reflected an emerging revolution in the field of American psychiatry.

The *DSM-III* discarded the psychoanalytical approach of the *DSM-I* and *DSM-II*, which relied primarily on theories of unconscious conflict being the cause of most expressions of psychopathology. The *DSM-III* wanted to achieve greater diagnostic reliability by creating a new approach to identifying mental disorders based solely on observable signs and symptoms. Prior to the *DSM-III*, disorders ranged along a spectrum from 'normal' to 'severe'. The *DSM-III* organized 'observable' signs and symptoms into discrete categories outlining the criteria for a particular disorder. By 2000, the *DSM-IV* had expanded to almost 1,000 pages and in 2013 the *DSM-V,* comprised of 974 pages, was published after six years in the making amid much criticism and controversy.

Among those who challenged the *DSM-V* were Robert Spitzer, the editor of the *DSM-III*, and Allen Frances, the editor of the *DSM-IV*. Their two primary complaints were the secrecy surrounding the process that determined what would be included in the new edition and the belief that by lowering thresholds for particular disorders, the *APA* was pathologizing behaviors that were previously considered appropriate or normal in response to the circumstances. They referred to this paradigm shift as the *"medicalization' of normal human emotions"*. In other words, in the absence of using a spectrum to assess symptoms and behaviors on a scale from 'normal' to 'severe'; we now run the risk of pathologizing and medicating what might not have previously met the criteria for 'severe' but is, instead, developmentally or situationally appropriate.

Having worked for several years with at-risk, under-served populations in my community; I have witnessed first-hand their extreme vulnerability and the significant impact that the *DSM* and the field of psychiatry can have on their lives. In order for insurance companies, including Medicaid, to be willing to pay mental health professionals so that individuals can receive treatment and services, there must be a documented diagnosis with a corresponding numerical code for billing purposes. Unfortunately, these diagnoses can negatively impact the lives of millions of people in the United States every day by influencing where they can live, what jobs they can hold and how their children will be educated. Because the *DSM* is also utilized by public housing authorities, school officials, lawyers, judges and prison officials; a mental disorder diagnosis could end up causing more harm than good.

While helping at-risk youth transition back into the community from correctional facilities, I was deeply disturbed to discover that all juveniles in the state of Virginia who are incarcerated are initially processed at the *Reception and Diagnostic Center* for psychiatric evaluation. Every child I worked with, without exception, had been given a diagnosis of a mental disorder and medicated before being assigned to a correctional facility. None of them, in my opinion, came close to meeting the criteria for their respective diagnoses. One can only conclude that containing a large population of adolescents within an over-crowded, privately-owned, for-profit, prison setting must be much more manageable if that population has been heavily medicated.

Since the first *DSM* was published in 1952, psychiatric diagnoses have increased significantly; leading to speculation by many experts in the field of psychology and psychiatry that many diseases are now being promoted by large pharmaceutical companies in their marketing campaigns in an attempt to increase sales.

Shyness made its debut in 1980 in the *DSM-III* as a psychiatric disorder that is now referred to as *'Social Phobia'*. By 1994, the *DSM-IV* was referring to it as *'Social Anxiety Disorder'*. Five years later, the FDA approved Paxil for said disorder and sales soared into the billions of dollars for *GlaxoSmithKline*. On July 2, 2012, *Glaxo* pled guilty to criminal charges and was fined three billion dollars for marketing *Paxil* for unapproved uses and failing to report drug safety information to the U.S. *Food and Drug Administration* (FDA). The settlement covers improper *Glaxo* practices from the late 1990s to the mid-2000s in which *Glaxo* offered kickbacks to doctors and sales reps to push the drug and helped publish a paper on *Paxil* in a medical journal that misrepresented clinical trial data.

As reported by *Time Magazine* on July 5, 2012:

❖ *Although the antidepressant Paxil is not approved for patients under 18, Glaxo illegally marketed the drug for use in children and teens, offering kickbacks to doctors and sales representatives to push the drug.*

❖ *A government probe was launched in 2002, and it was discovered that Paxil, as well as several other antidepressants, were no more effective than placebo in treating depression in kids. Indeed, between 1994 and 2001, Glaxo conducted three clinical trials of Paxil's safety and efficacy in treating depression in patients under 18, and all three studies failed to pass muster.*

❖ *One clinical trial, known as Study 329, found that teens who took the drug for depression were more likely to attempt suicide than those receiving placebo pills. Glaxo hired a company to prepare a medical journal article that downplayed Paxil's safety risks, including increased risk of suicide, and misrepresented data to trump up the positive results of the study. The article was published in 2001, falsely reporting that Paxil was an effective treatment for child depression.*

❖ *Prosecutors accused Glaxo sales representatives of using the article to promote the use of the drug for depressed youth. Sales reps invited prescribing psychiatrists to luxury resorts for "Paxil forum meetings" where they were treated to fancy dinners, sailing trips, spa treatments, and balloon rides.*

❖ *Reports of teens committing suicide while taking Paxil began surfacing in 2003, and the FDA discovered that 10 of the 93 Paxil patients in Study 329 had attempted suicide or thought about it, versus one out of the 87 patients on placebo. In 2004, the FDA added a black-box warning on the drug's label about the increased risk of suicidal thoughts in teens who take it.*

This now brings us to an even greater concern which makes the waters of the *DSM*, the *American Psychiatric*

Association (APA), and *Big Pharma*, so murky that any attempt to navigate it may cause us to collectively and completely lose our minds. However, let's do our best to push ahead in the hope that we may find some pharmaceutical intervention to ease the ever-increasing cognitive dissonance around what it is we're about to discover:

In 2006, a research paper out of the *University of Massachusetts* was published in the journal *Psychotherapy and Psychosomatics* entitled *"Financial Ties Between DSM-IV Panel Members and the Pharmaceutical Industry."*

The following is the **Abstract**:

Background: *Increasing attention has been given to the transparency of potential conflicts of interest in clinical medicine and biomedical sciences, particularly in journal publishing and science advisory panels. The authors examined the degree and type of financial ties to the pharmaceutical industry of panel members responsible for revisions of the Diagnostic and Statistical Manual of Mental Disorders (DSM).*

Methods: *By using multimodal screening techniques the authors investigated the financial ties to the pharmaceutical industry of 170 panel members who contributed to the diagnostic criteria produced for the DSM-IV and the DSM-IV-TR.*

Results: *Of the 170 DSM panel members 95 (56%) had one or more financial associations with companies in* the pharmaceutical industry. One hundred percent of the members of the panels on 'Mood Disorders' and 'Schizophrenia and Other Psychotic Disorders' had financial ties to drug companies. The leading categories of financial interest held by panel members were research funding (42%), consultancies (22%) and speakers' bureau (16%).

Conclusions: Our inquiry into the relationships between DSM panel members and the pharmaceutical industry demonstrates that there are strong financial ties between the industry and those who are responsible for developing and modifying the diagnostic criteria for mental illness. The connections are especially strong in those diagnostic areas where drugs are the first line of treatment for mental disorders. Full disclosure by DSM panel members of their financial relationships with for-profit entities that manufacture drugs used in the treatment of mental illness is recommended.

The following paragraphs are transcribed from *"Shrinks for Sale: Psychiatry's Conflicted Alliance"*, an article published by the *Citizens Commission on Human Rights* (CCHR), an international mental health industry watchdog:

❖ *In July 2008, the U.S. Senate Finance Committee requested that the APA provide accounts for all of its pharmaceutical funding. In March 2009, the American Psychiatric Association announced that it would phase out pharmaceutical funding of continuing medical education seminars and meals* *at its conventions. Despite its announcement, within two months, the APA accepted more than $1.7 million in pharmaceutical company funds for its annual conference, held in San Francisco. Within a month of the APA's announcement, its conflicts came under criticism again with the release of a study that found that 18 of the 20 members overseeing the revision of clinical guidelines for treating just three "mental disorders" had financial ties to drug companies. The three diagnoses generated some $25 billion a year in pharmaceutical sales.*

❖ *In June 2007, The New York Times reported that psychiatrists in Vermont and Minnesota topped the list of doctors receiving pharmaceutical company gifts and that this financial relationship corresponds to the "growing use of atypicals [new antipsychotics] in children." From 2000 to 2005, drug maker payments to Minnesota psychiatrists rose more than six-fold to $1.6 million. During those same years, prescriptions of antipsychotics for children under the state's insurance program rose more than nine-fold.*

❖ *With the U.S. prescribing antipsychotics to children and adolescents at a rate six times greater than the U.K., and with 30 million Americans having taken antidepressants for what psychiatrists admit is a pharmaceutical marketing campaign, it is no wonder that the conflict of interest between* *psychiatry and Big Pharma is under congressional investigation. ***

The APA is heavily steeped in a conflict of interest with the pharmaceutical industry since making at least 40 million dollars in sales of the *DSM*. The financial conflicts between psychiatrists involved with the *DSM-IV* and the *DSM-V Task Forces* are under scrutiny along with *Big Pharma's* influence on what disorders are included in the *DSM* since these disorders contribute to the current 25 billion dollars in annual anti-psychotic and anti-depressant drug sales in the U.S.

One of the most concerning expressions of this particular social experiment that I've witnessed during the past eleven years, is the increasing vulnerability of children to be diagnosed with *Attention Deficit Disorder* (ADD) and prescribed amphetamines because of their inability to conform to rigid and unrealistic expectations within the classroom.

In my opinion, this phenomenon has been perpetuated by a fear-based culture that took root in response to the Columbine school shootings which occurred in 1999. Prior to this unprecedented and unimaginable event, there was a greater willingness to assess child and adolescent behaviors on a scale that provided a context for what would be considered developmentally and situationally appropriate.

It is also my opinion that the pharmaceutical companies have knowingly taken advantage of this and contributed to this culture of fear by manipulating parents, teachers, administrators and pediatricians into believing that medicating a brain with stimulants during its most critical stages of development is the wisest course of action when the child's behaviors do not conform to the expectations of those in charge.

The following are excerpts from the *New York Times* published on December 14, 2013 on *"The Selling of Attention Deficit Disorder"* by Alan Schwarz:

❖ *Recent data from the Centers for Disease Control and Prevention show that the diagnosis had been made in 15 percent of high school-age children, and that the number of children on medication for the disorder had soared to 3.5 million from 600,000 in 1990.*

❖ *Profits for the A.D.H.D. drug industry have soared. Sales of stimulant medication in 2012 were nearly $9 billion, more than five times the $1.7 billion a decade before, according to the data company IMS Health.*

❖ *The rise of A.D.H.D. diagnoses and prescriptions for stimulants over the years coincided with a remarkably successful two-decade campaign by pharmaceutical companies to publicize the syndrome and promote the pills to doctors, educators and parents. The industry is now employing similar marketing techniques as it focuses on adult A.D.H.D., which could become even more profitable.*

- Behind that growth has been drug company marketing that has stretched the image of classic A.D.H.D. to include relatively normal behavior like carelessness and impatience, and has often overstated the pills' benefits. Advertising on television and in popular magazines like People and Good Housekeeping has cast common childhood forgetfulness and poor grades as grounds for medication that, among other benefits, can result in "schoolwork that matches intelligence" and ease family tension.

- Insurance plans, increasingly reluctant to pay for specialists like psychiatrists, are leaving many A.D.H.D. evaluations to primary-care physicians with little to no training in the disorder.

- Many doctors have portrayed the medications as "safer than aspirin," even though they can have significant side effects and are regulated in the same class as morphine and oxycodone because of their potential for addiction.

- Like most psychiatric conditions, A.D.H.D. has no definitive test, and most experts in the field agree that its symptoms are open to interpretation by patients, parents and doctors. The American Psychiatric Association, which receives significant financing from drug companies, has gradually loosened the official criteria for the disorder to include common childhood behavior like "makes *careless mistakes" or "often has difficulty waiting his or her turn."*

❖ *When federal guidelines were loosened in the late 1990s to allow the marketing of controlled substances like stimulants directly to the public, pharmaceutical companies began targeting the most impressionable consumers of all: parents.*

❖ *The Food and Drug Administration has repeatedly instructed drug companies to withdraw such ads for being false and misleading, or exaggerating the effects of the medication. Many studies, often sponsored by pharmaceutical companies, have determined that untreated A.D.H.D. was associated with later-life problems. But no science determined that stimulant treatment has the overarching benefits suggested in those ads.*

❖ *Many critics said that the most questionable advertising helped build a market that is now virtually self-sustaining.*

❖ *Today, 1 in 7 children receives a diagnosis of the disorder by the age of 18. As these teenagers graduate into adulthood, drug companies are looking to keep their business.*

During an interview with *Time Magazine* in 2012, Dr. Irwin Savodnik, an assistant clinical professor of psychiatry at the *University of California, Los Angeles*, summed it up best:

"The very vocabulary of psychiatry is now defined at all levels by the pharmaceutical industry."

* *See **Appendix A** for a list of individuals who have been under Senate Finance Committee investigation for the roles they played in furthering sales for Big Pharma in exchange for large monetary donations.*

Summary

❖ *Since the first DSM was published in 1952, psychiatric diagnoses have increased significantly; leading to speculation by many experts in the field of psychology and psychiatry that many diseases are now being promoted by large pharmaceutical companies in their marketing campaigns in an attempt to increase sales.*

❖ *The financial conflicts between psychiatrists involved with the DSM-IV and DSM-V Task Forces have been under Congressional scrutiny along with Big Pharma's influence on what disorders are included in the DSM, since these disorders contribute to the current 25 billion dollars in annual antipsychotic and antidepressant drug sales in the U.S.*

❖ *Of the 170 DSM panel members, 56% had one or more financial associations with companies in the pharmaceutical industry. One hundred percent of the members of the panels on 'Mood Disorders' and 'Schizophrenia and Other Psychotic Disorders' had financial ties to drug companies.*

❖ One in four children in this country between the ages of 13 and 18 has now been identified as suffering from an anxiety disorder.

❖ In 1985, half a million children in the United States met the diagnostic criteria for ADHD. Today it is estimated that 5 to 7 million children in this country now have this diagnosis.

❖ Sales of stimulant medication in 2012 were nearly 9 billion dollars, more than five times the 1.7 billion dollars from a decade before.

❖ Three and a half million children have met the criteria for a diagnosis of depression and a recent study showed a 600 percent increase in the diagnosis of pediatric bipolar disorder in children under the age of 13 within the last 10 years.

❖ The U.S. is prescribing anti-psychotics to children and adolescents at a rate six times greater than the U.K. and 30 million Americans have taken antidepressants for what psychiatrists admit is a pharmaceutical marketing campaign.

❖ *The most questionable drug company advertising has managed to successfully build a market that has become virtually self-sustaining.*

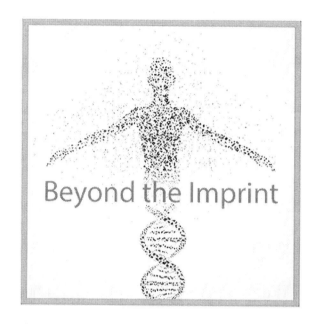

Beyond the Imprint

BEYOND THE IMPRINT

❖ *We are intimately interconnected with our environment and everything that inhabits it, which also includes the understanding that we can change what is outside of us by simply changing ourselves.*

❖ *As long as we are imprinted and conditioned to look outside of ourselves in order to identify who, and what, is causing us pain or pleasure; we will always be trying to manipulate and control our environment, and those in it, in an attempt to mitigate loss and minimize our suffering.*

❖ *In order to move beyond our unconscious reliance on our environment to reassure ourselves that we are safe and secure; we must begin to dissolve our wound imprinting.*

❖ *Our journey towards integration and wholeness requires that our attention be directed primarily inward to resolve whatever trauma imprinting and subsequent self-judgments we are defending against that reinforce our beliefs that we are not enough.*

❖ *Only then can we begin to experience the freedom to develop to our fullest capacity; Beyond the Imprint, towards self-actualization.*

What is Therapy?

Five years ago I was working with 9 year-old Gracie who did not want to go home when her father came to pick her up at the end of our session. Somewhat exasperated, he asked her why it was that he always had to 'drag' her to therapy, but whenever he came to get her she never wanted to leave. Without any hesitation, she responded:

"Therapy is like having to take a bath. At first you don't want to go, but once you're in it; you don't want to get out."

I keep this quote framed on the wall in my office not only as a reminder that we always have much to learn from the innate wisdom of our children, but also because Gracie isn't alone when experiencing some degree of anxiety and resistance prior to an upcoming session, and once there and settled in, would prefer to linger much longer than the allotted time.

So let's find out why therapy can often feel at first like having to take a bath.

When entering into the therapeutic experience with a trained and skilled professional, there will always be awareness on some level that if you commit to the process then your life, as you know it, will change. The prospect of change, in and of itself, will always be a source of some anxiety because the client is asking the therapist to take them on a journey into the unknown. Without realizing it, we have all unconsciously developed an array of coping mechanisms over the years in order to navigate and survive our environment, which includes the relationships we've formed. These coping mechanisms, often referred to as defense mechanisms, ensure that we minimize our feelings of pain, loss and anxiety in response to experiences of trauma and chronic stress so that we can continue to put one foot in front of the other and function according to the expectations of self and others. The irony is that eventually, over time, these defense mechanisms end up informing dysfunctional behavioral and relationship patterns that become the stumbling blocks which prevent us from experiencing the quality of life we truly desire. Therapy is an opportunity for the individual to increase their awareness around what is preventing them from having their preferred experience.

I once heard a story, which I refer to often when working with clients as an analogy to describe my particular style, and how I envision my role and responsibility as their therapist.

Someone once asked Michelangelo how he was able to carve the statue 'David'. He simply replied, "I just carved away what wasn't David."

Over the years I've developed the ability to listen with my 'third ear' and reflect back to the client what it is they communicate without even realizing it; essentially what is hidden between their words. When the defense mechanisms are down and there's less attention being given to auditing the self; the individual will begin to reveal how they truly feel and what they really believe. My job is to hear it and reflect it back to them. In doing so, I am essentially 'carving' away what isn't them. These aspects have been created as a means of self-protection in order to ensure their survival. By gradually 'carving' away who they aren't; who they really are and what they truly desire, begins to reveal itself.

Hopefully, therapy is a journey in which the individual is provided an opportunity to explore what unconscious assumptions/beliefs and dysfunctional behavioral/relationship patterns are getting in the way of them achieving the very things they've identified they would like to experience; which always, without exception, ends up being a happier and more joyful life filled with a greater sense of self, ease and fulfillment.

Summary

❖ *There will always be awareness on some level that your life, as you know it, will change once you commit to the therapeutic process.*

❖ *The prospect of change, in and of itself, will always be a source of some anxiety because the client is asking the therapist to take them on a journey into the unknown.*

❖ *Defense mechanisms ensure that we minimize our feelings of pain, loss and anxiety in response to experiences of trauma and chronic stress so that we can continue to function.*

❖ *Over time, these defense mechanisms end up informing dysfunctional behavioral and relationship patterns that become the stumbling blocks that prevent us from experiencing the quality of life we truly desire.*

❖ *Therapy is an opportunity for the individual to increase their awareness around what is preventing them from having their preferred experience.*

Who Benefits From Therapy?

The quick answer is pretty much everyone. Of course children under the age of twelve, in general, would be limited in their capacity to engage in any significant self-reflective work and would benefit more from some form of play therapy. I say 'in general' because once in a while I get to work with an eight or ten year old who would fit the description 'old soul' and, as such, has tremendous clarity and insight into themselves and others. But usually, if there's a need to work with young children; there exists some significant dysfunctional patterns within the family system and, in this case, it would be more effective to work with the whole family while placing much of the focus on the parents/primary caregivers. Exceptions to this would include adoption in which the child is currently living with a healthy family, but is still dealing with the effects of trauma imprinting from when they were with their family of origin, or some type of physical, mental, or emotional disability that is limiting the child's ability to function. Once the child has reached adolescence, emerging meta-cognition increases their capacity to participate in a process of self-reflection, allowing for a more dynamic therapeutic experience.

In exploring the question, *Who Benefits from Therapy?*, there are a few consistent and fairly common presentations that I have experienced over the years in my practice.

The first one represents the largest demographic that I work with and occurs when the parent identifies, often with help from school administrators, that something is wrong with their child and they would like my help in 'fixing' whatever that might be. The assumption on the parent's part is that if I do my job well and 'fix' their problem child, then the family as a whole can get back to the business of functioning in a healthier and more balanced way. What I've learned over the years is that nothing could be further from the truth, and even more intriguing, the identified 'problem' child always ends up being the healthiest member of the family.

The second presentation that I see often in my practice is when a spouse has identified that their marriage or partnership has become a source of great pain and suffering and is looking for my help in trying to either 'fix' the relationship or dissolve it. In order for there to be even a glimmer of hope in salvaging the relationship; both partners need to be equally motivated and committed to doing so. Personally, I've never experienced this. Without exception, one partner usually has one foot out the door long before they or their partner contacts me for assistance. My role as I see it is to help them achieve clarity around what they truly desire and to help them achieve it as gently and lovingly as possible.

The third presentation that makes up a significant part of my practice is the twenty-something year old who has achieved some degree of personal and professional independence for the first time in their lives and is beginning to notice that they have some unresolved *stuff* from childhood that seems to be 'blocking' their continued identity-formation, including their ability to form healthy and satisfying relationships. What I love most about working with this demographic is that they are, without exception, incredibly 'hungry' to learn and understand how to achieve mental, emotional and spiritual well-being in an effort to experience a much greater purpose in their lives.

The fourth and final presentation is the smallest demographic that I've worked with, but undoubtedly deserves a big mention considering that the most challenging transitions one will ever have to navigate occur at this stage of one's life. *Sexagenarians*, *Septuagenarians*, and *Octogenarians* represent individuals between the ages of sixty and eighty-nine. I like to think of an individual lifespan occurring in three trimesters, with each trimester spanning approximately thirty years.

The first trimester is all about identity formation. Depending on how secure and healthy your attachments were to your primary caregivers, you should be well centered and balanced with the knowledge of who you are by the time you reach your second trimester. This trimester is all about settling into your life plan in regards to career and family which is determined by how you see yourself and what makes sense for you. So your life plan could involve you being a stockbroker, married to an ex-Dallas Cowboys cheerleader who gives you three 'perfect' kids while living in Westchester, NY; *or* it could be backpacking indefinitely around the world with your current girlfriend or boyfriend while taking odd jobs when necessary to finance the trek while looking forward to the ceaseless unknowns that continue to reveal themselves around every corner and over every mountain range. It doesn't matter what your life plan is or how safe and predictable it is; it just needs to make sense to you.

By the time you reach the third trimester, you've begun your life review and are experiencing the impermanence of life, in general, as the concept of retirement begins to loom large on the horizon. Health and well-being becomes a greater concern because the body is now more vulnerable to manifest some type of disease expression. Children who had been a primary focus during the second trimester have launched themselves and are beginning to formulate their own life plan. Friends, colleagues and relatives you've known and loved for some time, including your own parents, are starting to deal with significant health issues and are beginning to transition beyond this lifetime.

Regardless of which demographic we're speaking of, they all have one thing in common. When it comes to beginning the therapeutic process, no one seeks out a therapist because they're feeling really good about themselves. On the contrary, everyone who comes to therapy does so because they're experiencing a significant amount of emotional pain and suffering that even well-honed coping mechanisms can no longer alleviate. Even with the understanding now that therapy is not exclusive to the severely, mentally ill and emotionally disturbed; there still lingers a stigma amongst the collective perception from when this was actually true. This could explain why the majority of people do not allow themselves to seek out this venue of support until after experiencing many years of suffering.

The most important thing to remember is that no matter what your age or identified problem; therapy can be the beginning of a dynamic journey into the self as a means to identify and achieve what your heart truly desires.

Summary

❖ *Almost everyone can benefit from a therapeutic process facilitated by a skilled, knowledgeable and competent practitioner.*

❖ *No one seeks out a therapist because they're feeling really good about themselves.*

❖ *Everyone who comes to therapy does so because they're experiencing a significant amount of emotional pain and suffering that even well-honed coping mechanism can no longer alleviate.*

❖ *Therapy can be the beginning of a dynamic journey into the self as a means to identify and achieve what your heart truly desires.*

Finding a Therapist

I will begin by saying that none of my clients have found me through advertising. I know this because I have never advertised my services. I did, however, create a website as a platform for describing to prospective clients who I was and what demographics and issues I work with. If you go there you will see that my home page includes an essay I wrote which addresses my concerns about our society's increased tolerance and advocacy for 'chemically restraining' our youth. I mention my training in, as well as the efficacy of, *Energy Medicine* as a means of healing the mind/body/spirit. There's a page devoted to Linus, my three year-old, 75lb Labrador Retriever who is a certified therapy dog and who joins me in sessions with clients as my co-therapist. You can also find a list of workshops that I offer as well as a brief bio that describes my education, training and the fact that I'm originally from Canada. A list of my other websites will tell you that when I'm not in session with clients, I am usually working on a number of graphic and photographic projects. And last but not least, there is a picture of my smiling face so you can better assess whether or not sitting across from me week in and week out might be a pleasant enough experience.

Other than that, you don't have anything else to go by that would help identify that working with me might actually be beneficial in achieving greater equilibrium in your life.

So then, what would be the best way to find a therapist who would be a good fit for you?

Based on my own experiences as both therapist and client, I can easily conclude that the best way to find a therapist, who would be more helpful than harmful, is to find one through someone you know and trust. All of my clients, without exception, were referred to me by another client or by a social worker who picked me specifically for a case because they believed it would be a good fit for the client.

Once you've been given the name of a reputable therapist by someone you trust, the next step is to make an initial appointment. I recommend that this appointment be largely driven by the client through a process of interviewing the prospective therapist. And here's essentially what you want to know before moving forward with the relationship:

What is their level of education in the field of mental health counseling and where did they receive it from?

Because you want to know that they have a broad knowledge base which should include sound academic research which they are able to draw information from that is relevant to, and helpful in, understanding your situation.

How long has he/she been practicing in the field of mental health counseling?

Because you want to know that they have had a fair bit of training and experience and that they are not experimenting on you.

How many clients do they currently have and how many hours do they work every week?

Because you want to make sure that they are not over-extended and exhausted; but rather, well-balanced and healthy in so far as they do not ask more of themselves than what is reasonable. Good therapists should be modeling healthy behaviors rather than practicing within a *"do as I say, not as I do"* framework.

If they have one, what is their area of specialization?

Because it may not prove helpful to go to a therapist who specializes in substance abuse issues if that is not your issue.

Have they ever been married or in a long-term relationship and do they have children?

Personally, I would be remiss in seeking advice and wise counsel from someone who has never had any experience with what it is they are providing advice on. To do so, would limit your therapeutic experience to an academic and theoretical framework, full of speculation. I also believe it is important to consider the age of the therapist. A twenty-three year old therapist will always have a limited capacity in working with an older client with a lot more life experience because their schemas will not have been developed beyond twenty-three years of life experience.

What do they like the most about their job?

Because you can tell a lot about a person by what they like most about their job.

What do they like least about their job?

Because you can tell a lot about a person by what they like least about their job. Also, keep in mind that their job involves working with you, so what they like least about it is going to affect you.

What do they do to renew their energy levels at the end of each day/week?

Because it's important to work with someone who is not exhausted or depleted. Being an effective therapist requires a tremendous capacity to be 'present' and to 'hold space' for the client no matter how traumatic the material is that is being excavated, processed and released.

And last but not least, but without doubt the most important question you could ever ask a prospective therapist:

Is he/she working on themselves? If so, in what way?

What exactly do I mean by that?

This is not a small subject because it addresses what it is, exactly, that draws an individual to practice their life's work in the field of mental health counseling.

Beyond the Imprint explores how an individual is 'imprinted' on a cellular level through their DNA lineages, their own personal experiences beginning at conception, as well as what was modeled for them and projected onto them by the people in their environments while growing up. All of this cellular 'imprinting' is what has unconsciously influenced perceptions, belief systems, defense mechanisms, behaviors and relationship patterns.

In short, when someone decides to make it their life's work helping others; it will always be an expression of how they were imprinted throughout childhood. In all likelihood, they would have had some early training in becoming the emotional flotation device for a primary caregiver. In all likelihood, they would have had some version of having the 'proverbial shit' knocked out of them that left a lasting impression in the very cells of their body. This mixed with the unconscious drive to provide for others what was not provided for them, creates a relationship dynamic between the therapist and the client in which the person they are really attempting to help or 'rescue', is themselves. Unless they are working very consciously and very diligently at combing through and excavating all of their own personal *stuff*; then they will have no awareness of this and, as a result, their *stuff* will always be in the room, and not so carefully tucked away. What's important to understand is that the issue is not with the fact the therapist's *stuff* is in the room because this is always going to be true. It's that the therapist is not aware that this is the case and will, without realizing it, always be defending that this is true; in their posturing, in the power dynamic that is inherent when this issue is prevalent, and in the style that they choose to work. This dynamic will, without exception, always limit their capacity to facilitate an effective and lasting change in the client's experience.

So how do you, the client, assess whether or not this is true? Try introducing this subject to your prospective therapist and wait for their reaction. If they strongly disagree and become extremely defensive; not only do you have confirmation that it is true, but also that they haven't even begun to consider that it's even necessary and appropriate to be working on themselves. The only question you need to be asking yourself at this point is; *"How on earth can someone take me to the places that I've resisted going to on my own, if they aren't able or willing to go there themselves? "*

Often, and usually in reference to me, my father would use the expression, *"There goes the blind leading the blind."* This would be an appropriate description of working with a therapist who is not working on themselves. So if you want an experience in which you come in every week and tell your story over and over again as a means to vent, get things off your chest and *'be heard'*; then whether or not your therapist is working on themselves would not be an issue for you. However, if you really want to have a very different experience as it relates to being in relationship with self and others; which, in turn, will influence the experiences you have, then you should be working with someone who is engaged in an exhaustive and ongoing inventory of themselves. Only then, can you truly be taken to the places that will result in profound healing and a very different quality of being.

Summary

❖ *The best way to find a therapist, who would be more helpful than harmful, is to find one through someone you know and trust.*

❖ *You want to confirm that the therapist has had extensive training and experience as well as a broad knowledge base that is relevant to your situation.*

❖ *Being an effective therapist requires a tremendous capacity to be 'present' and to 'hold space' for the client no matter how traumatic the material is that is being excavated, processed and released.*

❖ *Ensure that your therapist is engaged in an exhaustive and ongoing inventory of their own imprinting otherwise their capacity to facilitate an effective therapeutic process for you will be extremely limited because they can't take you where they've never gone themselves.*

The Therapeutic Relationship

I believe that the relationship between a client and a therapist is sacred. It is not unlike what an individual would expect to experience when seeking wise counsel from a pastor, a priest, a rabbi, a shaman or any spiritual teacher. And yet, in my opinion, it involves so much more. In addition to being a trusted confidante, one of the therapist's roles is to create a safe and sacred space that allows the client to connect with, and excavate, difficult, threatening and traumatic material in a way that does not overwhelm or further traumatize them. This takes incredible skill and intuitive abilities on the therapist's part which, ideally, is being expressed with tremendous reverence and compassion for the process at hand. I believe that very little long-term, significant change can occur for the client if the therapist is not able to express from the heart. Because of this, I believe that what makes this relationship the most sacred, is that in order for it to be dynamic and effective, it requires a great deal of intimacy.

Now I added an extra space between these two paragraphs to let my readers ponder a little longer on what it was I just said. I did this because I suspect that it will have set off some alarm bells in a few folks.

"Surely, she didn't mean intimacy?"

Yes, she did.

"Perhaps it's a typo."

Nope.

It's not.

I learned many years ago when studying with my non-clinical teachers that the heart is the highest frequency through which any of us can express while in a physical body. It is my premise, when making this statement, that very little healing can occur in the absence of a space or a relationship filled with heart.

Let's start by identifying that intimacy does not infer the absence of boundaries. When studying to become a mental health counselor and when taking the examination in your respective state to become licensed; much of the material is devoted to learning what the ethical guidelines are within the therapeutic relationship.

However, in order to become an effective 'agent of change', it's important to develop the ability to hang out very close to the edge of these guidelines without crossing over into forbidden territory. I credit my success in being able to do this with the fact that I am one of those therapists who is constantly working on themselves in an effort to bring as much awareness to the moment regarding how I might be getting in the way of the client's process in order to ensure that I don't.

Because of this I am able to work in a way that does not feel dry or scripted. Years ago, as a client, I worked with a couple of therapists addressing relationship issues who seemed to be operating exclusively from a *Cognitive Behavioral* framework. I'm assuming this to be the case because in both instances my husband and I, and years later, my partner and I, were literally given scripts to follow as a therapeutic intervention in response to the therapist identifying that we had 'communication issues.'

Not surprisingly, it proved most unhelpful as our 'communication issues' were just a symptom of some much deeper dysfunctional patterns which would have been more helpful to identify and address. As it turned out, these experiences helped inform my decision to become a therapist and perhaps figure out how to practice my craft in a way that might actually be helpful to someone desiring a different experience in their relationships and in their life.

Over the years, I have stopped counting how many times a client has unburdened a deeply held secret for the first time in one of our sessions. They could not tell their wife, their husband, their best friend or their pastor/priest/rabbi/shaman/spiritual teacher but for some reason they were able to tell me. I've come to understand that this level of intimacy is only possible when the therapeutic 'space' that is being 'held' for the client is filled with heart and absent of any judgment or conditions. This 'space', however, does not infer the absence of boundaries.

The most important boundary to be maintained involves the understanding of what happens when the therapist becomes 'inducted' into the client's dysfunctional patterns. Textbooks teach us about *transference* and *counter-transference* between a client and a therapist and identify it mostly as a bad thing that the practitioner would want to avoid at all times. This refers to the client engaging with the therapist as if he or she were the primary caregiver with whom the client has the most unresolved material. When the therapist is unaware that these projections are occurring and responds unconsciously by becoming defensive with their own projections or by needing to placate the client; it is at this point that the therapist has become 'inducted'. The job of the therapist is to help the client identify dysfunctional patterns and change them. In order to do this it is important that the therapist not participate in the dysfunctional patterns.

One of the most common forms of 'induction' that I have experienced is in working with individuals or families that generate and feed off of a lot of drama and chaos. It's very easy to get pulled into this because there is a very real and palpable, energetic vortex around chaos and drama. It will touch on and 'trigger' all of our cellular imprinting around survival. So when sitting with someone whose adrenals are becoming activated while telling their story about who did what to whom; it's hard *not* to notice, as a therapist, how easy it is for my adrenals to become activated. The trick is to just notice it without responding to it. And this is one example of what I was referring to in the previous chapter when I identified that the therapist's *stuff* is always going to be in the room. What's important is that we know it and not defend that it's true when engaged with the client regarding the client's *stuff.* After all, the client is paying us to focus on their *stuff.* So a perfect example of the therapist maintaining appropriate boundaries in this case is to ensure that they are in control of the session by not allowing the client to continue to 'spin' in their vortex of chaos and drama. This can be achieved with heart and loving-kindness. Boundaries are evidence of heartfelt, loving-kindness because they are, by their very existence, evidence that the self and the other are considered sacred and worthy of consideration.

In addition to expressing from the heart, intimacy requires that there be transparency in the relationship and transparency is best achieved when the therapist is able to be empathic. During the 1980's and '90's, an Italian neurophysiologist, Dr. Rizzolatti, discovered mirror neurons in the frontal lobes of the brain; which are neurons that 'fire' when we perform an action as well as observe the same action in others. Further research using fMRI's has demonstrated that this mirroring system is the neural basis of the human capacity for emotions such as empathy. Empathy is feeling and experiencing what the other is feeling and experiencing while always maintaining focus on, and directing attention to, the other. Being able to do this allows you to acknowledge and affirm the other person's experience on a much deeper level than is usually achieved in a casual, impersonal relationship.

Reverence, compassion and loving-kindness are all hallmarks of a sacred experience. Any relationship that occurs within this 'space' would be considered intimate. Maintaining this frequency within the therapeutic arena allows for the client to experience emotional safety in a way never before experienced in any other relationship. Only when the client feels this degree of safety can they allow themselves to drop their defense mechanisms and be truly transparent. Only then, when vulnerable and transparent, can any significant, long-term changes occur.

Summary

❖ *The therapist's role is to create a safe and sacred space that allows the client to connect with, and excavate, difficult, threatening and traumatic material in a way that does not overwhelm or further traumatize them.*

❖ *This takes incredible skill and intuitive abilities on the therapist's part which ideally, is being expressed with tremendous reverence and compassion for the process at hand.*

❖ *The therapist's job is to help the client identify and change dysfunctional behavioral and relationship patterns without becoming 'inducted' and part of the dysfunctional patterns.*

❖ *Therapeutic boundaries are evidence of heartfelt, loving-kindness because they are, by their very existence, evidence that the self and the other are considered sacred and worthy of consideration.*

❖ *Maintaining reverence, compassion and loving-kindness within the therapeutic arena allows for the client to experience emotional safety in a way never before experienced in any other relationship.*

❖ *Only when the client feels this degree of safety can they allow themselves to drop their defense mechanisms and be truly transparent, resulting in significant and long-term change.*

When Therapy isn't Helpful

There are three specific factors within the therapeutic arena that I believe, whenever present, greatly minimize the client's ability to experience any significant, long-term results. I doubt that these are the only factors that would minimize results, but in my estimation, based on what I've observed and experienced, they are probably the most common and influential.

The first factor would be what the client brings to the experience. This includes the understanding that everyone who seeks out this venue of support is going to have some degree of anxiety due to the awareness that they are embarking on a journey into the unknown and that their life, as they know it, is about to change. In order for this process to be successful, well-honed defense mechanisms will need to be surrendered in order to allow the therapist to take them to the places that they have resisted going for so long. I've come to understand that the extent to which the client has been traumatized or 'shattered' correlates directly to the degree of resistance that the he or she brings to the therapeutic experience. Resistance is one of the most common defense mechanisms and is informed exclusively by fear. It is important for the therapist to recognize this because this understanding should be informing the style and pace at which the therapist proceeds in order to not overwhelm or further traumatize the individual. However, sometimes the fear/resistance is so great that the client is unable to move beyond their story and the need to tell it over and over again. Part of the story always includes the need to continuously identify that the environment and certain individuals within it are responsible for their current situation. Consistent with this orientation is an over-reliance on the therapist or the 'expert' to 'fix' them. Very little progress can be made as long as the client holds strong to this position.

Such a position is largely determined by what has yet to be resolved from the original trauma(s), including the individual's emotional age at the time they experienced the traumatic event. It is this aspect, the younger version of his or herself, that has so much difficulty letting go and trusting that they are safe in the present moment. It is this younger version that has so much difficulty letting go of the need to blame others for whatever it is that they are experiencing that is undesirable and unwelcome. So even though I may have a 48 year old high-powered executive in front of me; I am also aware that his 6 year old self is making sure we don't move forward too quickly, if at all, into dangerous, unchartered and forbidden territory. My job is to increase his sense of safety and security so that he can relax and feel safe enough to begin to let go of his 'story' and allow himself to be exposed, transparent and vulnerable; to be truly 'seen' not as a victim, but as someone who has the capacity to change his experience without fear or resistance.

The second factor that minimizes the potential for long-term, significant changes in the client's life would be what the therapist brings to the experience. In the previous chapter, I identified the importance of working with someone who is continuously attentive to their own healing process in order to ensure that they bring the greatest degree of awareness to their practice. This quality of awareness creates a resonance between the therapist and the client because it is inherently understood that the client is merely a reflection, and the process that the therapist is facilitating is not unlike any other process they facilitate for any other client, including the one they facilitate for them self. A skilled therapist knows to direct the 'responsibilities of change' back to the client while offering him or herself as a 'guide' and 'facilitator'. This awareness is what fosters empathy and compassion for the client, the absence of which ensures that there will always be a power dynamic between the therapist and the client. In the absence of working on the self or identifying that there is even a need to; the therapist will always be posturing unconsciously within an *"I'm okay, you're not"* attitude; which is always being reinforced by the need to be seen as the 'expert'. This style of posturing always goes hand in hand with a strong attachment, on the therapist's part, to a particular outcome. After all, they are the 'expert' and how much progress the client does or doesn't make will be perceived by them as a measure of how good they are as a therapist. The problem with this approach is that it has as much, if not more, to do with meeting the therapist's emotional needs as it does the client's. Another measure of this dynamic being present is when the therapist insists on pathologizing the client's behaviors because as the 'expert', it now becomes their job to 'fix' whatever they have identified is wrong. When present, this dynamic will always serve to reinforce the client's victimology because, once again, the 'authoritative figure' that they are in relationship with, has complete control over their experience. Within such a relationship dynamic the client will never be able to resolve the trauma(s) that continue to inform their beliefs, behaviors and relationship patterns.

The third and final factor refers to the style of therapy being proffered. I am aware that the style and manner in which I acquired my clinical training that has influenced my practice will always carry an inherent bias on the subject of "what works". However, my identification of "what doesn't work", is largely determined by my own experiences as a client and what my collective clientele over the past eleven years has shared with me. As a result, I would have to conclude that most of what is being proffered as therapy doesn't result in any long-term, significant changes for the client. I also believe that this collective experience further reinforces the ongoing stigma associated with therapy not being a reliable or meaningful venue for any significant healing. This will always be true as long as it is a place where people go to vent and project blame onto family members, or talk in great length about what it isn't about. The majority of clients whom I've worked with, and who span the entire range of demographics, have experienced some trauma within the therapeutic realm. Over time, I came to understand that this was not an anomaly, but rather an experience more common than one would imagine given the inherent oxymoronic nature of such an experience.

A few years ago, a client came to me for issues related to grief. The first thing she identified was that she was referred to me when the therapist she had been seeing for the past thirteen years retired. My immediate response was to identify that if we were still working together thirteen years from now then that would be evidence of me not doing my job very well. As it turns out, her previous therapist had allowed her to come in for thirteen years and essentially talk about what her issues weren't about. I understood this to be the case because by our third session I was able to identify that her grief issues had very little to do with the recent passing of her beloved cat and where we really needed to be focusing our attention was on her significant history of domestic violence, abuse and incest within her family of origin, throughout her entire childhood. She acknowledged that this was not an area she had ever been able to explore with her previous therapist.

By our fourth session, she had decided to work with an animal communicator instead of me to help her with her unresolved grief. I had no judgment regarding her inability to journey down this difficult path at this time. However, I also believe that she had been strongly conditioned by her previous therapeutic experience to avoid the difficult material as much as possible and that a big part of this conditioning was evidenced by her over-reliance and extreme dependence on her therapist over the course of their thirteen year relationship.

Creating co-dependent relationships with your clients is not an uncommon occurrence and another perfect example of when the therapy becomes the problem. Becoming part of the problem is something that a therapist would want to avoid as much as possible all of the time. In order to do this, he or she should, at all times, be directing their attention within in order to ensure that the therapeutic framework in which they are operating from is not reinforcing the client's, or the family's, dysfunctional patterns.

Summary

Three specific factors within the therapeutic arena that can greatly minimize the client's ability to experience any significant, long-term changes:

❖ **What the client brings to the experience:**

Sometimes the fear/resistance is so great that the client is unable to move beyond their story and the need to tell it over and over again. Consistent with this orientation is an over-reliance on the therapist or the 'expert' to 'fix' them.

❖ **What the therapist brings to the experience:**

In the absence of working on the self or identifying that there is even a need to, the therapist will always be posturing unconsciously within an "I'm okay, you're not" attitude which is always being reinforced by the need to be seen as the 'expert'.

❖ **The style of therapy:**

Creating co-dependent relationships with the client is not an uncommon occurrence and another perfect example of when the therapy becomes the problem.

Compassion Fatigue

Let's begin by first identifying that I do not believe that there is such a thing as *Compassionate Fatigue*. What makes my identification even more interesting is that I'm writing this particular chapter from my oceanfront room at the beach because I am taking a much needed and overdue break from my practice in order to replenish my own energy levels. So I am very familiar with the quality of fatigue that can accumulate over time when working with individuals in distress. In which case, what exactly is it that I could be referring to when making such a potentially unpopular claim?

Compassion Fatigue is often described as second-hand trauma; an extreme state of chronic tension and preoccupation with the suffering of those being helped to the degree that it is exhausting and traumatizing to the therapist. I do believe that this experience exists and that it is extremely prevalent within the mental health counseling field and other 'helping' professions. I just don't believe that it occurs as a result of practicing compassion. Simply put, if one were truly practicing compassion one would not be fatigued, 'burned out' or traumatized as a result of doing this kind of work. In fact, it would be a very different kind of experience for the practitioner, one that is far more equanimeous.

I chose to focus my attention on this subject in an attempt to bring awareness to a quality of 'helping' that will always be overlooked if we continue to participate in the mainstream identification and definitions of the experience known as *Compassion Fatigue*. This very different quality of 'helping' can actually create a greater potential for change and healing while allowing the therapist to increase their own capacity to facilitate such an experience for their clients.

So let's take a closer look at what compassion really is and what needs to be occurring in order to truly fulfill the definition of what it means to be compassionate. For this understanding I've chosen not to refer to Mr. Wikipedia or Ms. Merriam-Webster but, instead, to draw from my own experiences with the Buddhist monks and other wisdom teachers who have taught me through their actions, not their words, what it really means to practice compassion.

Compassion is an expression which truly originates from the heart. We learned in a previous chapter that heart frequency is the highest frequency through which we can express while in physical form. The key to this understanding is to be able to differentiate between what is heartfelt and what is not. My experience is that most expressions of what we, as a collective, call heartfelt or loving, are not. Being compassionate requires a greater understanding of the difference between the two.

Compassion can only be experienced when one is detached. Detachment is the opposite of being attached and has nothing to do with being disconnected; quite the opposite. It is the ability to be fully present, in the moment, regardless of what is occurring in that moment. It is the ability to accept and absorb what is happening, in the moment, with love, reverence and gratitude even when what is occurring is difficult. It is not controlling, judging, grasping, inserting, adjusting, organizing, projecting, defending, identifying or resisting. It is the ability to allow yourself to feel and fully sensate what is occurring; to let it move through you and not get stuck in your mind or your body; to have the experience and be complete when the experience is complete. Only when one is completely detached can love and compassion be truly expressed.

I am not, by any means, suggesting that this is easy to put into practice which is why I'm writing this chapter while on a much needed break at the beach. I fully expect to be working on this for many lifetimes to come. What I am saying, though, is that it's important to begin to stretch and move towards this understanding and orientation in order to increase our capacity to create real significant and lasting change in our own lives as well as in the lives of those who seek us out for assistance in minimizing their distress and healing their trauma.

While in service to others within the therapeutic arena, there is a strong tendency to be extremely attached to outcomes. These attachments are what create the experience referred to as *Compassion Fatigue*. The fatigue, exhaustion and second-hand trauma develop from the conscious and unconscious identifications that what is occurring in the moment needs to look different and it is the therapist's responsibility to ensure that it does. Therefore, the best place to begin fostering real compassion is by learning how to let go of our attachments to outcome.

What fundamentally gets in the way of our ability to let go of our attachments to a particular outcome is that all of our relationships are being influenced by our unconscious attempts to fulfill our own emotional needs. The degree to which this occurs correlates directly to the extent that they were not fulfilled during our most formative years by our primary caregivers. The tension that we feel in response to working with individuals who are distressed comes from the dissonance that we experience when sitting with their trauma and the subsequent judgments and projections that occur in an unconscious attempt to deflect the awareness that we are sitting with our own reflection. In other words, sitting with trauma touches in on our own trauma imprinting. Subsequently, any attachment we have to the others experience or situation looking different is really coming from our inability to accept and come to terms with our own situation(s), past and present. This brings us back full circle to the understanding in which the therapist is always trying to 'rescue' themselves through the work they facilitate with their clients despite any altruistic thoughts they may be harboring to the contrary. The fatigue is a result of the chronic tension experienced when the therapist keeps 'bumping' up against their own *stuff* and defends against the experience by projecting onto the client that the client's experience needs to look different. By doing so, the therapist never has to deal with the discomfort and anxiety stemming from their own unresolved trauma imprinting.

Judgment and resistance is the tension that creates the experience of fatigue. Fatigue and compassion do not co-exist because compassion is the state of non-judgment and complete acceptance. Compassion can be achieved by practicing detachment. Evidence of compassion being present within the therapeutic relationship is determined by the practitioner's ability to accept what is occurring in the moment. This, in turn, is limited by the practitioner's ability to accept their own experiences and to the extent in which they are engaged in their own healing process. Looking within to heal, resolve and accept whatever has happened in the past that was distressing, uncomfortable and traumatic dissolves whatever memory is still being held onto in the physical body. The trauma imprinting dissolves in response to one's own ability to accept rather than defend their experiences and subsequent wounding. This, in turn, increases one's capacity to practice true compassion, which is the only authentic expression of love; the act of complete and total acceptance. The degree to which this can be extended to another is always going to be determined by one's own ability to be compassionate with the self. Only then, can the other be truly 'seen' because how they show up is no longer conditional on their ability to meet our needs.

Summary

❖ *While in service to others within the therapeutic arena, there is a strong tendency to be extremely attached to outcomes.*

❖ *Fatigue, exhaustion and second-hand trauma develops from the conscious and unconscious identification that what is occurring in the moment needs to look different, and it is the therapist's responsibility to ensure that it does.*

❖ *Sitting with trauma touches in on the therapist's own trauma imprinting. Subsequently, any attachment they have to the client's experience or situation looking different is really coming from their inability to accept and come to terms with their own experiences.*

❖ *The best place to begin fostering real compassion is by learning how to let go of our own attachment to outcome.*

❖ *Evidence of compassion being present within the therapeutic arena is determined by the practitioner's ability to accept what is occurring in the moment.*

❖ *Detachment is the ability to accept and absorb what is happening in the moment with love, reverence and gratitude even when what is occurring is difficult.*

❖ *Only when one is completely detached can love and compassion be truly expressed.*

What is Healing?

The question *"What is Healing?"* is one I find increasingly provocative. At first glance it seems almost rhetorical, which would be one of the reasons I thought it deserved closer consideration. Another reason is that given what I do for a living, this is a subject that is always present in the room when working with clients since the expectation would be that if I'm any good at what I do, then I should be able to facilitate a 'healing' experience for them.

I'm also going to suggest that what rarely gets discussed within the therapeutic venue is what exactly the operational definition of 'healing' is within the context of the client's or patient's experience. What I've come to understand is that the expectation usually involves the dissipation and dissolution of whatever emotional, mental or physical symptoms that may be causing pain and discomfort for the individual. However, what I've come to believe, as a result of my own personal experiences, those of my family and friends and those whom I sit with, is that the process of 'healing' has very little to do with the eradication of symptoms.

Within the framework of the allopathic model of conventional, Western medicine, the focus is almost always about the suppression and eradication of the patient's symptoms. This approach is what has allowed the global pharmaceutical industry to grow from generating four hundred billion dollars in 2001 to as much as a trillion dollars in 2014 with North America being responsible for more than forty percent of those revenues. *The World Health Organization* (WHO) now estimates that one third of sales revenue, more than three hundred billion dollars annually, is spent on marketing pharmaceutical products, which is about twice as much as what is spent on research and product development. Consequently, the WHO has identified that the continued pressure to generate sales at this level has led to *"an inherent conflict of interest between the business goals of manufacturers and the social, medical and economic needs of providers and the public to select and use drugs in the most rational way."*

The reason it's important to acknowledge these demographics and statistics is because they reflect the greatest influence in our culture's unconscious conditioning on the subject of *"What is Healing?"* They also determine how we attempt to get our emotional and physical needs met through a course of action that is designed to 'numb' our pain without any significant inquiry as to what the underlying factors are that influence our disease expressions and subsequent symptoms.

When I was thirteen years old I was diagnosed with what doctors identified was an extremely aggressive, auto-immune disorder and suggested that unless my symptoms were controlled through very aggressive pharmaceutical protocols; it was highly probable that I would be in a wheelchair by the time I was eighteen years old. Looking back from the vantage point of forty years later, which will always include the contextual framework of *"had I known then what I know now"*, I would have taken issue with that prognosis.

By the time I was twenty-five years old, I had been treated by a large number of physicians; all experts in their respective fields of practice. During the twelve years following my initial diagnosis, I was hospitalized eight times for a total of seven months within four different hospitals. I received monthly *gold salt* injections and was prescribed 1,000 mg of *naproxen* and 2,000 mg of *entrophen* every day as well as long-term doses of *prednisone*. During this time, the side effects from the toxicity of what was being prescribed to me began to impact my internal organs and when I attempted to address my concerns with my physicians they refused to acknowledge that these other emerging issues were related at all to the toxicity from the pharmaceuticals I had been prescribed for thirteen years. It was at that point that I realized I would rather be in a wheelchair than on a transplant list.

From the perspective of thirty years later, I can now be grateful for the physicians who were not able to move beyond the linear framework of their training and conditioning when responding to my needs. Most physicians are not adequately trained to assess the underlying causes of complex, chronic diseases and to apply strategies such as diet, nutrition, bodywork and exercise to treat and prevent these illnesses. As it turned out, my doctors were no exception. However, their rigidity propelled me into a holistic model of health care which, in turn, evolved into a metaphysical, spiritual and healing journey that continues to nourish me and shape all of my creative and clinical work, including this book.

From a clinical perspective, I have observed that the same conditioning present in allopathic medicine exists in the field of mental health counseling as expressed through the *Diagnostic Statistical Manual* (DSM-V) and the field of psychiatry. Behaviors that are considered 'abnormal' are easily pathologized and quickly medicated which, in my opinion, is just another example of suppressing the symptoms and 'numbing' the pain in response to what makes us uncomfortable. Instead, I believe that a very different inquiry needs to happen in order to even be in the 'ballpark' of what could be considered a 'healing' experience. If we can accept that all behaviors make perfect sense when you understand the schemas that are influencing them and that schematic development is primarily determined by early childhood experiences beginning at conception; then we can begin to understand at what level the inquiry ideally needs to take place in order to realize any significant changes in our experience.

As long as the primary focus is on eradicating the symptoms; then we are operating from a superficial level of inquiry. Symptoms are a reflection of something occurring at a much deeper level and reflect an underlying imbalance within the whole system; mental, emotional, physical and spiritual. Unless we address the underlying imbalances that perpetuate the disease expression, the patient or client will remain unhealthy regardless of whether or not they are taking medication to suppress the symptoms. In addition, the toxicity of the medication always comes with side-effects that, over time, create more serious health concerns which almost always end up eclipsing the initial complaint.

My fifty-eight year old brother was diagnosed with the same auto-immune disorder as I was but much later in life. His rheumatologist prescribed a daily protocol of 20mg of *prednisone* as far back as 2009 and a few years later added the biologic *Enbrel* to his repertoire of medications. Since then I have watched him show up to family functions looking increasingly unwell and in September of 2014, when we were gathered at the beach for a family reunion there was no doubt in my mind that he was headed for a significant health crisis. In July of 2015, he was hospitalized with a number of infections, including an antibiotic resistant strain of *MRSA*. At the time, I was reminded that one of the many common side effects of *Enbrel*, as identified by the manufacture, is a 'near-fatal' infection.

During the eight months he was hospitalized, he spent multiple weeks in the ICU during which time he was in a coma, had numerous surgeries, including an amputation, chronic pneumonia and a heart attack. At 6'4" he weighed, at best guess, no more than 125 pounds. He's never been able to be weaned off of the *prednisone* because every attempt to do so has resulted in his adrenals and other vital organs shutting down. For twelve months he received daily infusions of the strongest antibiotics known to medicine to address the *MRSA*. He had a neurologist, cardiologist, podiatrist, rheumatologist, infectious disease specialist, pulmonary specialist and pain management specialist. Both my brother and his wife looked to all of these doctors for guidance as to how to proceed, if at all, in their efforts to keep him alive. The problem with this approach is that, despite what we might see on medical TV shows, the doctors are remiss in providing any kind of a prognosis and, instead, focus primarily on procedures and interventions to ensure that the patient keeps breathing. None of them consulted with each other, but they all seemed equally perplexed as to how he got to this critical juncture at such a young age. After being resuscitated, a *DNR* was put in place only to have it removed a few days later because there was a difference of opinion on the subject between two of his doctors. Given a choice, my sister-in-law wanted to believe in the doctor who thought my brother still had a chance, understandably so.

The most concerning part, is that my brother's ongoing recovery and rehab, eighteen months later, is the result of his immune system having been significantly compromised due to the pharmaceuticals prescribed by his rheumatologist during the previous six years. Once he entered the hospital with the initial onset of infections, the antibiotic infusions further compromised whatever immunity he may have still had. There was no protocol put in place to strengthen his immune system and restore the necessary probiotics in his gut since no such protocol exists within the allopathic framework. As a result, the next six months bore witness to the gradual breakdown of his entire physical body in response to what was put in motion years ago on the recommendation of his rheumatologist.

As long as our health care providers assess our well-being exclusively through the lens of their individual specializations informed by whatever symptoms are presenting, our overall health and longevity will always be compromised. Doctors are well-trained to treat symptoms but are not trained to address the underlying imbalances that perpetuate the disease expressions. One analogy I read recently on this subject described this approach as similar to taking the batteries out of a smoke detector instead of trying to find the fire.

Healing is not the absence of symptoms. Healing is the experience of bringing the entire system into balance. This requires a much deeper inquiry and understanding of what created the imbalance in the first place. Symptoms are just evidence that such an imbalance exists just like the smoke alarm going off is evidence that there's a possible fire in the house. It's much easier to take the batteries out of the smoke alarm in the same way it's much easier to take a handful of pills each day in order to 'numb' the pain and discomfort; but unless a much deeper inquiry is made, the house will eventually burn down.

Healing Through the Lens of the Imprint

In addition to our DNA being our 'blueprint' for life; how we develop in utero in response to our mother's stress levels, the degree of trauma we experience at birth, how securely we are able to attach to our primary caregivers, and how nurturing our childhood environments are; appear to be the most important factors influencing our development and the degree of health and stability we are able to optimize throughout the course of our lifetime. While our genetic makeup determines our vulnerability to manifest particular physical, emotional and mental disease expressions; it is the degree of stress and trauma that we experience throughout life that determines the likelihood of whether or not we will manifest such an expression and how early on we will do so in our development.

Healing is a journey towards integration and wholeness which requires that our attention be directed primarily inward to resolve whatever trauma imprinting and subsequent self-judgments we are defending against that reinforce our beliefs that we are not enough. In order to dissolve the imprint, we must dissolve all judgment. Anything we judge that is outside of us reinforces whatever judgments we have against ourselves because being in opposition to anything reinforces our imprinting and subsequent dysfunctional patterns that emerge from that imprinting. These patterns not only take the form of relationship dynamics, but also mental, emotional and physical disease expressions we are genetically predisposed to.

Our judgments continue to reinforce an orientation of opposition in which we are always looking outside of ourselves to get our needs met, which also includes our subsequent reactivity when we perceive that they are not. This, in turn, ensures that we will continue to cycle through our wound imprinting making us increasingly vulnerable to manifest whatever disease expressions we are genetically predisposed to. As long as we continue to look outside of ourselves in order to identify who and what is causing us pain or pleasure; we will always be trying to manipulate and control our environment and those in it in an attempt to mitigate loss and minimize our suffering. The extent to which we continue to cycle through these patterns will always be determined by the extent to which our needs were met during our most critical stages of development since appropriate environmental stimulus in response to our needs validated our right to exist at the cellular level.

Healing is a journey towards self-love and self-acceptance in which we will have infinite and endless opportunities to let go of our judgments. Our level of self-care is always a reflection of our relationship with the self and reveals the degree of self-acceptance and self-love we are able to embody in the moment. Our capacity to love and accept ourselves will always determine our capacity to love one another just as my capacity to love my brother will always be limited by my capacity to accept what has happened to him.

I believe that the greatest gift he has ever given to me is this experience because if I can accept his process, including his unimaginable, prolonged suffering at the hands of a deeply flawed model of health care that he and his wife, along with millions of other individuals, place their faith in daily; then I believe that much of the trauma imprinting within me that resonates with this experience including how he imprinted me while we were growing up, will be dissolved.

So, in conclusion, I would have to say that healing is a profound journey that requires a tremendous amount of courage, faith, vulnerability, trust, humility, surrender and gratitude through which we will always have the opportunity to expand into fuller expressions of mental, emotional, physical and spiritual balance.

Summary

❖ *Symptoms are a reflection of something occurring at a much deeper level and reflect an underlying imbalance within the whole system; mental, emotional, physical and spiritual.*

❖ *Healing is not the absence of symptoms. Healing is the experience of bringing the entire system into balance. This requires a much deeper inquiry and understanding of what created the imbalance in the first place.*

❖ *Unless we address the underlying imbalances that perpetuate the disease expression, the patient or client will remain unhealthy regardless of whether or not they are taking medication to suppress the symptoms.*

❖ *While our genetic makeup determines our vulnerability to manifest particular physical, emotional and mental disease expressions; it is the degree of stress and trauma that we experience throughout life that determines the likelihood of whether or not we will manifest such an expression.*

❖ *Our judgments ensure that we will continue to cycle through our wound imprinting, making us increasingly vulnerable to manifest whatever dis-ease expressions we are genetically predisposed to.*

❖ *Healing is a journey towards integration and wholeness which requires that our attention be directed primarily inward to resolve whatever trauma imprinting and subsequent self-judgments we are defending against that reinforce our beliefs that we are not enough.*

❖ *Our level of self-care is always a reflection of our relationship with the self and reveals the degree of self-acceptance and self-love we are able to embody in the moment.*

❖ *Healing requires a tremendous amount of courage, faith, vulnerability, trust, humility, surrender and gratitude through which we will always have the opportunity to expand into fuller expressions of mental, emotional, physical and spiritual balance.*

Energy Medicine

Energy Medicine is a branch of alternative medicine that embodies the holistic phenomena that the mind and the body are deeply interconnected. The body's energy anatomy is as complex and multi-layered as its physical anatomy in which electromagnetic energies inform the infrastructure of the physical body. The health of those energies in terms of flow, balance and harmony is reflected in the health of the body. Conversely, when the body is not healthy, corresponding disturbances in its energies can be identified and re-balanced. Emerging scientific research and technology reveals how electricity, magnetism and light affect molecules and cells; providing new insights into the efficacy of *Energy Medicine* as an alternative approach to bringing all aspects of our being into balance.

Research has identified that at the time a traumatic event is experienced by the individual, their nervous system is overwhelmed by the amplitude and the enormity of the experience. Unable to effectively process and regulate in response to the event, which is experienced at the deepest level of survival instincts; the trauma, with all of its physical, emotional and psychological components and implications, is essentially 'flash-frozen' in time; imprinting the individual on a cellular level in the physical body. Often, when stressed, the individual will regress emotionally to the age that the trauma was experienced and the nervous system will become dysregulated around the cellular memory of survival having hung in the balance at that particular point in time. The anxiety in the present, in response to whatever stimulus is in the current environment, can be experienced as intensely as it was during the original trauma. Having studied animals in the wild under similar conditions, researchers have identified that the animal's ability to 'shake off' the experience through involuntary physical shaking and movements allows their nervous system to fully process and release the event. It has been observed that animals that are unable to do this will die once they return to their natural surroundings. It is my belief that most, if not all, emotional and mental disorders stem from the individual's inability at the time of the original trauma to allow the nervous system to fully process the event. In the present, *Energy Medicine*, bodywork and movement helps support and facilitate the nervous system's ability to process and release old traumatic cellular imprinting, allowing for a more regulated response when stressful stimulus presents itself in the individual's current experience.

Therapeutic modalities such as *Fluid Dynamic Cranial Sacral Therapy* and *Rolfing* have identified these cellular imprints as *inertia fulcrums* that exist in the fascia interrupting the flow of *qui* (chee). *Inertia fulcrums* can often manifest as a variety of physical symptoms and pain presentations which will ultimately lead to chronic, disease expressions. The nature of these symptoms, from one individual to the next, is determined by a person's genetic pre-dispositions as well as unconscious beliefs created about the self through environmental imprinting during the early, formative years of childhood development. Accessing these modalities helps release the *inertia fulcrums* specific to the individual's experiences; resulting in a greater ease and flexibility of emotional, mental and physical expression.

Massage Therapy is an important healing modality because it is important to be touched. Over time, years of emotional, physical and psychological imprinting from unsafe events, relationships and environments will create the perception that it is unsafe to be in our body. Most people are unaware of how much time, or to what degree, they have dissociated from the body. This is an unconscious attempt by the individual to avoid feeling the pain associated with traumatic or stressful events. For those who experienced chronic stress throughout childhood made up of a stream of events that seemed to lack a definitive beginning and end; learning how *not* to occupy the body was unconsciously developed as a means of survival. Psychotherapy should include helping the individual to 'ground' in the physical realm more fully despite the emotional and physical pain that might initially be experienced. *Massage Therapy* can be a gentle and effective way to support this part of the healing process. For individuals with a history of physical and sexual abuse, it is particularly helpful in assisting the individual to move through deeply held shame and guilt imprints relating to all matters of physical pleasure and pain.

Neuro Kinetic Therapy is a sophisticated form of manual therapy that combines motor control theory and manual muscle testing. The science of motor control theory states that the motor control center in the cerebellum stores all the coordination patterns of the body. It is directed by the limbic system and the cerebral cortex to not only create movement patterns (such as when a baby learns to stand), but also to create substitute movement patterns when we are injured. When a muscle is inhibited for whatever reason, the motor control center will find a substitute muscle to perform the function. If this pattern is allowed to remain in the motor control center, dysfunction and pain will follow. By applying light pressure that the client then resists, the practitioner can evaluate the strength or weakness of each muscle, revealing the sources of injury and retraining the client's body to remove the compensatory patterns; thereby reprogramming the body at the neural level. *Neuro Kinetic Therapy* is an excellent modality in rehabilitation and manual therapy because it not only identifies the cause of pain and dysfunction, but also corrects it very quickly and painlessly.

Meditation and *Prayer* through guided visualization, deep breathing and focused intention; include health benefits such as lowered blood pressure, stimulation of the body's immune system, stress release and enhanced emotional well-being, including increased self-esteem, relaxation and optimism.

Homeopathy is an alternative medical system that was developed in Germany more than 200 years ago using natural substances from plants, minerals and animals. It is a safe, gentle and natural system of healing that works with the body to relieve symptoms, restore itself and improve overall health. It is based on two rules of nature called the *Law of Similars* and *The Law of Minimum Dose. The Law of Similars* states that *"like cures like,"* or that a medicine can cure a sick person if it can cause a similar sickness in a healthy person. *The Law of Minimum Dose* states that the lower the dose of the medication, the greater its effectiveness. The homeopath regards symptoms as the body's healthy attempt to restore itself to balance. That is why a homeopath will choose a remedy that supports the symptoms rather than a remedy that opposes them or suppresses them as in conventional Western medicine. With the correct homeopathic remedy there are no side effects and a person is restored to health naturally.

Acupuncture is an ancient form of *Traditional Chinese Medicine* (TCM) for balancing the flow of energy or life force known as *Qi* or *Chi* (chee), which flows through pathways (*meridians*) in your body. The acupuncturist identifies blockages to the energy flow and opens up the pathways to increase circulation. This is done by inserting small needles into the skin at specific energy points along the meridians.

Floatation Therapy or *Restricted Environmental Stimulation Therapy* (REST) uses floatation tanks which are filled with a salt/water mixture warmed to ambient body temperature. The salinity of the water enables an effortless suspension, resulting in sensations of hovering in a gravity-free environment. This magnesium-rich water gets into the body's musculature system through trans-dermal infusion which releases tension by allowing the body to drain itself of lactic acid and cortisol. As the body relaxes, the floater's nervous system and mind relax as well. After thirty minutes of relaxation, the floater's brain realizes that there is no sensory input for it to process and becomes quiet and still. The serenity and peace achieved through floating is the same sensation that meditators often have after training for months. Floatation therapy has been studied at great length by the academic and scientific communities. To date, there have been over 250 studies done that support the effectiveness of the floatation tank's ability to induce deep relaxation. Studies have shown that floating in mineral-infused warm salt water, free from the stimulation of sensory input, decreases the floater's production of cortisol while increasing endorphins. Floating offers a peaceful and protected environment that restores the mind and body.

Reiki is a Japanese practice that trains practitioners to access Universal healing energy. This ancient modality is passed on from teacher to student and is an easily accessible form of energy healing. In the early 1980s, Dolores Krieger, R.N., created an American version called *Therapeutic Touch*. She introduced this aspect of healing energy to thousands of nurses.

Qigong is an ancient Chinese health care system that integrates physical postures, breathing techniques and focused intention. The word *Qigong* (Chee Gung) is made up of two Chinese words. *Qi* (chee) is translated to mean the life force or vital-energy that flows through all things in the Universe. *Gong* (gung) means skill that is cultivated through steady practice. Together, *Qigong* (Chee Gung) means cultivating energy. It is a system practiced for health maintenance, healing and increasing vitality. Practices vary from the soft internal styles such as *Tai Chi* to the external, vigorous styles such as *Kung Fu*. However, the slow gentle movements of most *Qigong* forms can be easily adapted by all age groups, including the physically challenged.

Flower Essences are an extremely subtle and effective form of energy medicine based on homeopathic principles which helps the individual 'peel' through the layers of imprinting, patterns and belief systems created by chronic stress and trauma that are no longer useful for continuing development. Blends for my clients are custom made on an ongoing basis in order best meet their needs at any given time in their healing process.

Below is a series of comments from a few of my clients describing their experiences following their first blend of *Desert Flower Essences*:

"Mental preoccupation is fleeting compared to its dominance even a year ago. It has only been since I began taking the essences that I am no longer head-centric but have found how to center myself in my heart and, when mindful, I put myself there. As an indicator of recent change, I have a colleague at work describe me as the guy who doesn't let things bother him and he sees me leading the way to a more relaxed atmosphere in the office."

"I've been waking up easier, without dreading my day. I managed to leave my awful job where I've been for two years. I haven't felt as angry, and I've been getting along with my dad a bit better because I've been finding it easier to stay calm. My dreams have been a bit more positive and I've had fewer nightmares."

"As I drove the kids to school it was a very surreal experience. At times it felt like the equivalent of a computer virus as these drops seem to have been given a backdoor path to my emotional core and were rattling my inner emotional self. There was a voice that was telling you "f-you" for having gotten past the defenses."

"Although I am very confident using alternative methods and medicines for mental, physical and spiritual health, I was skeptical of the effectiveness of flower essences. However, after the first day of use, I noticed a profound change in how my mind

was working. What is usually a constant state of chatter slowed to stillness and I found myself better able to focus on things that matter, a significant decrease in anxiety and a dramatic change in the way I perceive time. When the blend was revealed to me at the end of the bottle's use, it was obvious that the changes I experienced were a direct result of taking the essences."

"This blend has helped me become much more stable and confident. I'm more honest with myself and others and I'm trying to incorporate into my life what I believe is healthy for me. I've noticed less of a tolerance for those who prefer to find bad qualities in others and fixate on them. I feel open and much more willing to be vulnerable. I have become clearer about what exactly I want to do. For the most part I feel much more settled and comfortable with who I am and who I'm becoming."

During the past thirty years I have relied exclusively on *Energy Medicine* for my health care needs utilizing all of the modalities listed above at one time or another. This is a preventative model of health care that excludes the need for any pharmaceutical interventions; relying on diet, exercise, and natural supplementation to keep the three aspects of my being: body, mind and spirit, in balance and more fully integrated. As a result, my mental, emotional and physical well-being continues to improve every year, allowing me to experience greater harmony, stability and enjoyment within a gentle, loving and more balanced lifestyle.

Summary

❖ *Energy Medicine is a branch of alternative medicine that embodies the holistic phenomena that the mind and the body are deeply interconnected.*

❖ *The body's energy anatomy is as complex and multi-layered as its physical anatomy in which electromagnetic energies form the dynamic infrastructure of the physical body.*

❖ *The health of those energies in terms of flow, balance and harmony are reflected in the health of the body. Conversely, when the body is not healthy, corresponding disturbances in its energies can be identified and re-balanced.*

❖ *Emerging scientific research and technology reveals how electricity, magnetism and light affect molecules and cells; providing new insights into the efficacy of Energy Medicine as an alternative approach for bringing all aspects of our being into balance.*

On Forgiveness

All of the chapters in this book reference core, central themes specific to the **BTI** modality that I have stitched together over the years during all of the sessions I have facilitated for my clients. One of those central themes includes the understanding that what is reinforcing the fundamental 'split' in our individual and collective psyches is our unconscious participation in the dualistic paradigm that has shaped our schemas and influenced all of our beliefs and perceptions about ourselves and the world we inhabit.

Beliefs stemming from participation in this paradigm include the understanding that we are either 'good' or 'bad' depending on whether or not we make the 'right' or 'wrong' choices. Evidence of whether or not we made the 'right' or 'wrong' choice is often identified by whether or not those choices caused an 'injury' to self or others. We learn this quickly and early on in life because the voices of authority that surround us; our primary caregivers, teachers, ministers, politicians and the media, are quick to point out when the choices we make are considered either 'bad' or 'wrong'. As a result, we learn in the earliest stages of development, through these projections and their subsequent imprinting, how to judge ourselves and others; which includes the need to say *"I'm sorry"* and to ask for forgiveness for our perceived, injurious actions.

These beliefs continue to reinforce the self-judgments that are at the root of all of our disease expressions and subsequent suffering. Much of the focus in the initial sessions I facilitate for my clients is about 'unlearning' all of this conditioning in order to begin the healing process of integrating those aspects of the self that are separate from, and in opposition to, each other, as a result of these projections and subsequent, self-imposed judgments.

When we move beyond the dualistic paradigm and its inherent conditioning, there no longer exists the duality of 'right/wrong', 'good/bad', or the need for 'punishment/redemption'. Beyond dualism is a very different understanding of what we refer to as forgiveness. To further explore these concepts and help increase our understanding and awareness on this subject; I have transcribed the following article entitled, *On Forgiveness*. It was written by Yasuhiko Genku Kimura, who is a philosopher, cosmologist, Buddhist priest and scholar, and is an author in the fields of philosophy, ethics, science and business:

"The spiritual action that is forgiving is a transformational movement of human consciousness. Forgiveness ultimately means to attain to the state of consciousness in which the act of forgiving as such is rendered unnecessary.

When you are unforgiving you are simultaneously playing the victim and the judge. You feel convinced that you are right about your judgment and justified about your victimhood. When you feel convinced that you are righteous and justified, it is well-nigh impossible to give up your position of a victim and judge, for you do not see any compelling reason or feel any impelling desire to give it up.

The only problem is that you are bound to experience suffering. Although you feel self-righteous and self-justified, suffering is inherent in unforgiveness because it contains emotional pollutants such as anger, resentment, and sorrow, which beget unceasing internal friction, conflict, and disharmony.

When the victim is the righteous judge who decides the verdict, the verdict is a foregone conclusion -- that the perceived perpetrator is guilty and to be condemned. When you are unforgiving of yourself, you feel victimized by your own victimhood and therefore the real perpetrator exists ultimately elsewhere outside of you and is other than you.

Victim consciousness is the default mode of human consciousness while ego-logical consciousness is the default program. The human ego thrives on being self-righteous. Hence forgiveness is for many people extremely difficult. They would rather continue to suffer from anger, resentment, or sorrow so long as they can derive an ego-logical pleasure from feeling self-righteous and self-justified.

You have not yet forgiven yourself or others because in your subjective scale the pleasure that you derive from the state of unforgiveness outweighs the suffering that you experience. In fact, as G.I. Gurdjieff used to say, suffering is the last thing that people are willing to give up, for the human ego subsists on generated internal friction and no human experience generates internal friction more than, and as surely as, suffering.

What does it mean to forgive? To forgive means to give up your self-righteousness for what is truly right. To forgive means to give up your victimhood for self-responsibility and authenticity. To forgive means to give up your psychological dependency or co-dependency for spiritual independence and sovereignty. To forgive means to give up the negative pleasure of your suffering for the positive joy of living.

Forgiveness requires a transformational shift in attitude. We say that we want to forgive but in truth we don't want to forgive, for with forgiving we have to give up the presumption as well as the pleasure of moral self-righteousness and existential self-justification — two of the primary pillars that support the evanescent edifice of the human ego.

Therefore, unless you self-generate a will to transcend an ego-logical human existence, you will stay unforgiving for the rest of your life to the degree to which your ego demands for its subsistence.

Forgiveness does not imply condonation or consent. When someone commits an unjust action upon you or loved ones, in forgiving him, you are not condoning or overlooking his responsibility nor are you consenting or acquiescing to his action.

Forgiveness has nothing to do with the thoughts and actions of others but only with yourself – your authentic, higher self which is the seat of love and is your inner heaven. Forgiveness arises when you gain the light of insight that so long as you remain unforgiving, you are bound to condemn yourself to the inner hell of your own making.

The spiritual act of forgiveness comes from the state of spiritual independence, sovereignty, and freedom. Forgiveness implies knowing that your authentic self is independent of, and free from, thoughts and actions of others – understanding that your inner well-being is uncontaminated by, and immune from, any kind of negative external influences.

"How can I forgive?" This very question reveals a division, a dichotomy, a distance, between a 'you' who wants to forgive and another 'you' who does not, and between 'you' who is the victim and another human being against whose action 'you' are the judge. No resolution, no forgiveness is possible for the 'you' who asks this question from the level of consciousness in which this dichotomy exists.

Ultimately to forgive means to hold the whole of humanity within yourself as yourself. Forgiveness means to give light for darkness, to give love for hatred, and to give awareness for ignorance. To forgive means to hold nothing as external and uphold everything as internal to yourself. Therefore, to forgive is to be free."

Summary

❖ *Beliefs stemming from participation in the dualistic paradigm include the understanding that we are either 'good' or 'bad' depending on whether or not we make the 'right' or 'wrong' choices.*

❖ *Evidence of whether or not we made the 'right' or 'wrong' choice is often identified by whether or not those choices caused an 'injury' to self or others.*

❖ *We learn this quickly and early on in life because the voices of authority that surround us; our primary caregivers, teachers, ministers, politicians and the media, are quick to point out when the choices we make are considered either 'bad' or 'wrong'.*

❖ *As a result, we learn in the earliest stages of development, through these projections and their subsequent imprinting, how to judge ourselves and others; which includes the need to say "I'm sorry" and to ask for forgiveness from 'the other' for our perceived, injurious actions.*

❖ *These beliefs continue to reinforce the self-judgments that are at the root of all of our disease expressions and subsequent suffering.*

❖ *When we move beyond the dualistic paradigm and its inherent conditioning; there no longer exists the duality of 'right/wrong', 'good/bad', or the need for 'punishment/redemption'.*

Grief

The following is an extremely concise, psycho-educational overview on the subject of grief from the Western therapeutic perspective:

Most, if not all, clinical descriptions of grief are specific to the loss of a loved one and the process of bereavement that follows that loss. The diagnostic criteria as outlined in the *DSM-IV* (Diagnostic Statistical Manual) acknowledges that grief is extremely painful and a normal process following the death of a loved one, but that eventually the bereaved individual should adjust to a new and different life.

In addition to the process of bereavement, grieving can also be in response to the loss of other things such as a relationship, job, home, or anything else the individual might have valued. Symptoms of grief can include loss of appetite, sleeplessness, guilt, poor concentration, shortness of breath, restlessness, anxiety, intense sadness and tightness in the throat. It is expected that, over time, the wound associated with the loss will begin to heal and the individual would be able to resume their normal daily activities and experience more prolonged periods of happiness associated with those activities.

The *DSM-V*, which is the 2013 update to the *DSM-IV*, has identified a syndrome referred to as *PGD* (Prolonged Grief Disorder), which applies to individuals whose grief is persistent and disabling; so much so, that it threatens the individual's self-identity and security, making it impossible to envision any future filled with happiness, meaning or purpose. Studies have shown, however, that pathologizing grief can actually complicate the recovery process and prolong negative symptoms, which is why so much controversy surrounded the inclusion of *PGD* (Prolonged Grief Disorder) in the *DSM-V*.

There are many styles of grieving and experts agree that no one style is right or wrong. Whether it involves outward displays of emotion and the need to be supported by others, or more mental, problem-solving expressions in response to the loss; one style is not better than the other or more appropriate. What is important to acknowledge is that coping with loss is extremely difficult and we all have individual patterns and outlets for our grief.

In 1969, Swiss psychiatrist, Elisabeth Kubler-Ross, identified five stages of grief in her book, *"On Death and Dying"*. Motivated by a lack of material on the subject at the time, and her extensive experience working with patients in *Hospice*, she developed a model that became widely accepted by the general public despite the majority of research never being able to consistently support its validity. In response to this claim she later identified these stages as five common experiences related to any loss that could occur in any order and manner of progression:

Denial

During the first stage, the reality of the loss is questioned. A person might believe there was some sort of mistake such as a mix-up or an incorrect diagnosis.

Anger

Those in grief may begin to cast blame or ask questions like "Why me?", or become angry with the deceased e.g. "They were so selfish to take their own life!"

Bargaining

The individual may attempt to bargain as a way to avoid the cause of grief. For example, after receiving a terminal diagnosis, they might plead: "I will eat healthier, I'll quit smoking, and I'll do everything right if I can just get better."

Depression

During the fourth stage, the grieving enters a period of depression. They may lose motivation for living and isolate themselves.

Acceptance

The individual comes to accept the loss; although there may still be pain. During this stage there is a sense of calm and a resumption of normal life activities.

The following is my understanding of grief based on my own personal healing journey and my experience working with clients during the past eleven years:

I often use the analogy that the healing process we embark on is one in which we are always attempting to 'peel' away the infinite layers of our unconscious cellular imprinting that we were encoded with during the most critical stages of our early development in which we were overwhelmed by events and circumstances that had our sense of survival hanging in the balance.

I believe that our imprinting provides the only context in which we can truly understand what grief is and what is actually occurring when we grieve. Grief is a deeply held emotional response to a cellular memory being touched on by stimulus in our current environment that resonates with that memory. In order for this to 'ring true' as an accurate context for understanding what grief is, it's important to further distinguish what grief is not.

Grief is not denial. Nor is it anger, bargaining, depression or acceptance. Denial and anger are defense mechanisms. Bargaining is an attempt to control a situation that is perceived to be out of your control which would also classify it as a defense response. Depression is a mood disorder caused by chemical (neurotransmitter) imbalances in the brain, resulting in physical responses such as sleeplessness and loss of appetite that can lead to increased isolation and decreased energy and activity.

I often describe depression as the experience of having numerous, heavy, wet blankets on top of you rendering you completely immobile. It's not something you can think or feel your way out of, nor is it a grief response. In fact, the state of depression is the absence of being able to grieve at all. Acceptance, on the other hand, is the ability to be in harmony with whatever is occurring which is the absence of any defense mechanisms and a prerequisite for being able to even begin the grieving process.

Over the years I've observed consistent patterns in myself and my clients in which expressions of anger are far more prevalent as a response to stimulus in the environment touching in on the cellular imprinting of our trauma/loss memories. This makes perfect sense since anger is an extremely empowering response to something that feels threatening. I believe it's why most of us get stuck in this place of extreme reactivity which is disproportionate to whatever is happening in the moment because it activates an unconscious cellular memory from our past in which the threat and subsequent overwhelm was quite real. So we defend ourselves to the extent we were unable to at the time of the original trauma.

Defense mechanisms such as denial, anger and bargaining are patterns of resistance in response to whatever is happening in the moment that resonates with cellular memory of a time and a place in which we experienced our survival hanging in the balance. When we peel the layer of resistance away, we come to fear. This makes perfect sense considering that all of our imprinting is essentially *'flash-frozen'* cellular memory encoded in the frequency of fear. Had we not been afraid and overwhelmed at the moment of the original trauma, we never would have held onto the experience as a physical memory at the cellular/molecular level. Instead, we would have fully processed the experience throughout our entire nervous system and moved on, much like animals do when faced with overwhelming and potentially life-threatening situations in the wild.

So what does this have to do with grief?

Well, from my perspective, pretty much everything.

Defense mechanisms are patterns of resistance that have us in opposition to whatever is happening in the moment, in our environment, that resonates with a cellular memory of a time and a place from our past in which we felt threatened. We resist the experience because we are attempting to protect ourselves from being compromised or diminished in any way. Underneath all resistance is fear, but we prefer not to be in fear because that has us feeling much more vulnerable in response to the perceived threat. So rather than be vulnerable, most of us unconsciously choose anger as a reflexive response to the perceived threat. Anger is a defense mechanism, a form of resistance, and underneath all resistance is fear.

So what do you suppose we will find when we look underneath all expressions of fear?

What we find is what we've all been resisting from the moment we began defending ourselves.

We find grief.

The whole entire healing process I facilitate for myself and my clients is directed towards getting to this exact place. It is a place of total surrender in which all of the defense mechanisms we have so carefully honed over the years are dropped. We don't judge these mechanisms; quite the opposite. We give gratitude for our wisdom and fortitude for having unconsciously crafted such effective defenses that ensured our continued survival over the years. And we give gratitude for having finally arrived at a place that we have resisted going to for so long.

This resistance, I believe, comes largely from a deep misunderstanding of what it really means to grieve, and years of social and cultural conditioning that reinforced the misunderstanding.

Grief is not a process. Nor is it a feeling. And it does not have stages. Grief is not a sign of weakness, but rather an expression of incredible strength and courage. It is an expression that comes from very deep within in response to letting go.

Letting go of what?

Letting go of the fear of what might happen if we stop defending ourselves.

Letting go of the fear of what might happen if we allow ourselves to be vulnerable.

Letting go of the fear that we might become totally consumed by what we've never allowed ourselves to feel.

For most of my life I resisted letting go with every fiber of my being. My Celtic lineage as reflected in my own name, Catherine Michele Francis O'Connell, ensured that I would be able to aptly defend any threat that might present itself. It did not, however, ensure that I would avoid more than my fair share of trauma imprinting before reaching adolescence. As a result, being vulnerable was never an option for me in an unconscious attempt to ensure my continued survival into adulthood.

So you can only imagine my surprise to discover very late in life that the key to healing all of my trauma imprinting, subsequent imbalances and disease expressions, rested in my ability to put down my weapons and my shield; to let go and allow, and to trust that in doing so, not only would I survive, but I would actualize more than I could ever imagine was possible.

Grief is not so much an expression in response to what is happening in the moment. Instead, I believe that most of what the Western therapeutic perspective describes as grief is actually a trauma response. Grief is actually an expression of a memory that has been deeply buried in our respective psyches regarding our own self-identity at a particular time and place in our personal history. What is happening in the moment resonates with a memory of who we once were when the memory of a particular event from our past occurred. When that memory gets touched in on, so does a number of other awareness's that were prevalent at that time regarding our ongoing identity formation; including what we believed to be true and possible about ourselves, those we loved, and our future.

So when a loved one dies, I believe that grief is not just a response to their continued absence in our lives, but also a response to the recognition that the relationship we had with that person will never actualize its full potential. Even when it's a parent who's lived a long and fulfilling life; what we grieve is what was never able to be spoken between us before they left. What is grieved is the awareness that the capacity to be in a truly loving and intimate relationship absent of any dysfunctional relationship patterns was never realized. It's that loss that we grieve; what it wasn't and the loss of what it could have been had the circumstance of life been different. When it's someone who has died prematurely, we grieve not only what will never be realized in our relationship with that person but also what they will never become. We grieve on their behalf.

Therefore, I believe that grief is simply an expression of the loss of potential of who we thought we would become, including our dreams, aspirations, beliefs and hopes for what had yet to unfold for us. Simply put, grief is an expression of the loss of who and what we did not become; what we once thought was possible, but were unable to actualize due to circumstances beyond our control.

This understanding also helps to explain why there was such a strong collective grief response to the recent passing of such musical icons as David Bowie and Prince. It's an experience that feels much more personal than the situation would suggest because, after all, only a small percentage of people actually knew them personally, and yet, millions of people grieved their passing as if they had. That is because their music became a huge archetypal imprint during our most formative stages of development and, therefore, had great personal meaning and significance as a thread in the tapestry that helped form our individual identities.

These memories are deep stirrings and glimpses of what we once believed to be true about ourselves. Our grief is simply the acknowledgment of the loss of potential for the person who we once were and who we thought we would become. I have yet to meet anyone, including myself, who would have written their life story exactly as it unfolded.

"We must be willing to let go of the life we planned so as to have the life that is waiting for us."

–Joseph Campbell-

Our ability to grieve is essential in being able to dissolve our imprints. There are no detours. In order to move beyond our imprinting towards a more integrated, balanced and authentic expression of the self, we must be able and willing to let go and grieve the only loss we can ever truly grieve; the loss of ourselves.

This quality of grief is almost indescribable. It is gentle and nourishing and poignant beyond description. It is a salve that soothes the heart and soul; full of grace, gratitude and profound love for having finally found the courage to let go. It is the place of complete transparency. It is our inner heaven. Only from this place, is it possible to truly know ourselves and one another. Only from this place, is it possible to truly love ourselves and one another.

Summary

❖ Grief is an expression of a memory that has been deeply buried in our respective psyches regarding our own self-identity at a particular time and place in our personal history.

❖ Grief is a deeply held emotional response to a cellular memory being activated by stimulus in our current environment that resonates with that memory.

❖ When that memory becomes activated, so does a number of other awareness's that were prevalent at that time regarding our ongoing identity formation, including what we believed to be true and possible about ourselves, those we loved and our future.

❖ In order to move beyond our imprinting towards a more integrated, balanced and authentic expression of the self, we must be able and willing to let go and grieve the only loss we can ever truly grieve; the loss of ourselves, the loss of who and what we did not become; what we once thought was possible but were unable to actualize due to circumstances beyond our control.

Gratitude

*"Piglet noticed that even though he had a very small heart,
it could hold a rather large amount of gratitude. "*

- A.A. Milne -

Heart frequency is the highest frequency that can be expressed in this dimension while in a physical body. *Gratitude* is an aspect of the heart and its profound expression. All of my spiritual teachers, without exception, have acknowledged that without *Gratitude*, healing does not occur. My own experiences have taught me that this is, in fact, quite true.

Our religious conditioning has largely taught us to use prayer as a petition to God by focusing on what it is we don't have and asking for it. The problem with this approach is that Quantum Physics has already taught us that we will continue to manifest what it is we focus on. So if we focus on 'lack', then that is what we will continue to manifest.

Gratitude is, instead, the experience of acknowledging everything we do have that we are incredibly grateful for beginning with the fact that we are still here on the planet, in a body, and breathing. For a lot of us that is a remarkable accomplishment and something to be incredibly grateful for.

Gratitude is a posture of acceptance having arrived at a place in our lives in which the primary focus is on 'abundance' rather than 'lack'. To focus on 'lack' is a posture of non-acceptance because the focus is always on what isn't okay; what we're essentially in opposition to. Being able to maintain a posture of acceptance in response to whatever is unfolding even when it is extremely difficult, is the key to healing from our trauma/wound imprinting.

To assist in the process of healing within the frequency of *Gratitude* I am sharing a prayer I came across a number of years ago which I use often to align with all of the profound blessings I continue to experience in my life. In fact, this is the only prayer I recite because it says everything I could possibly imagine there is to say on the subject of being infinitely grateful for the profound healing that comes from being deeply interconnected with the natural world, as well as the awareness that there is no separation between any living thing, despite our conditioning that tells us otherwise.

Surprisingly, this prayer was not written by a theologian, a guru or a saint, but rather a political cartoonist from Australia:

We Give Thanks

We give thanks for places of simplicity and peace.

Let us find such a place within ourselves.

We give thanks for places of refuge and beauty.

Let us find such a place within ourselves.

We give thanks for places of nature's beauty

and freedom, of joy, inspiration and renewal,

places where all creatures may find acceptance

and belonging. Let us search for these places:

In the world, in ourselves, and in others.

Let us restore them. Let us strengthen

and protect them and let us create them.

May we mend this outer world according to

the truth of our inner life and may our souls be

shaped and nourished by nature's eternal wisdom.

\- Michael Leunig -

Summary

❖ *Heart frequency is the highest frequency that can be expressed in this dimension while in a physical body.*

❖ *Gratitude is an aspect of the heart and its profound expression.*

❖ *Being able to maintain a posture of acceptance in response to whatever is unfolding even when it is extremely difficult, is the key for healing from our trauma/wound imprinting.*

❖ *Healing does not occur without Gratitude.*

He said, "You become. It takes a long time. That's why it doesn't happen to people who break easily, or have sharp edges, or who have to be carefully kept. Generally, by the time you are Real, most of your hair has been loved off, and your eyes drop out and you get loose in the joints and very shabby. But these things don't matter at all, because once you are Real you can't be ugly, except to people who don't understand."

- The Velveteen Rabbit -

Beyond the Imprint (BTI) heralds a new paradigm of thinking within the field of mental health counseling that is beyond the duality of our unconscious conditioning. Quantum Physics is beginning to replace the mechanistic view of Newtonian Physics and is teaching us with every new discovery that we are intimately interconnected with our environment and everything in it. This includes the understanding that we can change what is outside of us by simply changing ourselves.

The goal of **BTI** is for the therapist to facilitate a safe, therapeutic experience in which the client is able to explore, identify and dissolve imprinting at the cellular level that has distorted self-identity and informed dysfunctional behavioral and relationship patterns throughout the course of their lifetime. Only then, will the client be able to actualize their true self and increase their capacity to manifest what it is they truly desire.

The following pages describe the **BTI** modality and include a brief synopsis of the **BTI** therapeutic process:

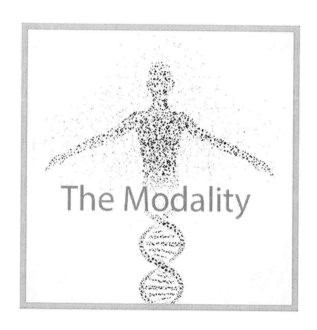

The Modality

THE IMPRINT

❖ *All of our thoughts, beliefs, perceptions, behaviors and relationship patterns have been shaped and informed by our respective DNA lineages and all of our experiences beginning at conception in the form of cellular memory referred to as 'imprinting'.*

❖ *Prenatal, perinatal and childhood experiences which should include appropriate environmental stimulus and responsiveness to our needs not only prevents distress, but also ensures that the limbic brain which receives and processes sensations, feelings and emotions 'imprints' these experiences as cellular memory in the body, validating our right to exist.*

❖ *If these experiences are less nurturing and more painful, our limbic system begins to 'imprint' these experiences on the cellular level as distorted expressions of love.*

❖ This sets us up to recreate these experiences in a cyclical fashion throughout life, informing chronic dysfunctional relationship patterns in an unconscious attempt to get our physical and emotional needs met.

❖ Our DNA may be the blueprint of life, but it turns out that our environment is what influences our genetic functioning, including our thoughts, feelings and beliefs in response to our experiences.

❖ How we develop in utero in response to our mother's stress levels, the degree of trauma we experience at birth, how securely we are able to attach to our primary caregivers and how nurturing our childhood environments are, appear to be the most important factors influencing development and future generations.

CONCEPTION

❖ *Imprinting begins at the moment of conception through the collective DNA of our respective lineages and their accumulative cellular memories, including trauma. This explains inter-generational patterns and expressions of behavior.*

❖ *At the moment of conception we are implanted in our very first environment; making us vulnerable to imprinting by whatever stressors our mother is being exposed to and her response to those stressors.*

❖ *As a result, our sense of safety and security begins to be encoded as cellular memory before we are even born.*

CHILDHOOD

❖ *Imprinting continues throughout childhood during one of the most vulnerable and critical stages of development.*

❖ *What is projected onto us and modeled for us by our primary caregivers is being influenced by their own respective and unresolved imprinting, which has been reinforced by centuries of social and cultural conditioning.*

❖ *Our schemas develop around this conditioning, which informs all of our beliefs and perceptions about our self, others and our environment, including the unconscious need to control or be controlled in order to feel safe and secure.*

❖ *The fact that we are the only organisms on the planet that are aware that our time in this physical body is finite is what makes us receptive and vulnerable to this conditioning.*

❖ *We unconsciously participate in the belief that we must conform to this conditioning in order to ensure our survival.*

ADOLESCENCE

❖ As children develop, they begin to model the existential angst that comes from their inability to conform to the conditioning inherent within the paradigm of our social and cultural conditioning.

❖ It begins with emerging adolescence and the dawn of meta-cognition when the individual begins to experience conformity as an equivalent to death.

❖ Without realizing it, they are defending their right to exist beyond the boundaries and confinement of this conditioning that projects onto them that their inability to conform is evidence of some inherent flaw that will limit their ability to be successful in getting their physical and emotional needs met throughout the course of their lifetime.

❖ What is being reflected back to them from their environments is negating them and challenging their ability to be in integrity with themselves in response to the distorted messages and unrealistic expectations being projected onto them.

❖ *Adolescence trying to function within the paradigm of this conditioning is a perfect storm which is why this stage of development is often defined by drama and crisis.*

❖ *If we, as adults, were able to recognize the degree to which we are influenced by our own imprinting and subsequent conditioning, we would be much better equipped to parent, teach and mentor this most critical and dynamic stage of development.*

❖ *Our teenagers are our 'truth tellers' and we have much to learn from them if we could only allow ourselves to listen and accept them without feeling the need to defend our position.*

ADULTHOOD

❖ *Conformity is how we have been conditioned to participate in this false sense of security which results in us being out of integrity with ourselves.*

❖ *On a deep, unconscious level we are aware of this and this awareness largely informs our suffering.*

❖ *We abdicate 'the self' by continuing to show up in the world in accordance with the expectations of others which is reinforced by their projections and our reflexive need to defend ourselves in response to those projections.*

❖ *We become imprisoned through fear of what other people will think of us. In an effort to mitigate loss, we participate in the collective conditioning that has us constantly relying on our environment and those who inhabit it to reflect back to us that we exist and are safe, secure, loved and accepted.*

BEYOND THE IMPRINT

❖ *We are intimately interconnected with our environment and everything that inhabits it which also includes the understanding that we can change what is outside of us by simply changing ourselves.*

❖ *As long as we are imprinted and conditioned to look outside of ourselves in order to identify who, and what, is causing us pain or pleasure; we will always be trying to manipulate and control our environment and those in it, in an attempt to mitigate loss and minimize our suffering.*

❖ *In order to move beyond our unconscious reliance on our environment to reassure ourselves that we are safe and secure, we must begin to dissolve our wound imprinting.*

❖ *Our journey towards integration and wholeness requires that our attention be directed primarily inward to resolve whatever trauma imprinting and subsequent self-judgments we are defending against that reinforce our beliefs that we are not enough.*

❖ *Only then can we begin to experience the freedom to develop to our fullest capacity; Beyond the Imprint towards self-actualization.*

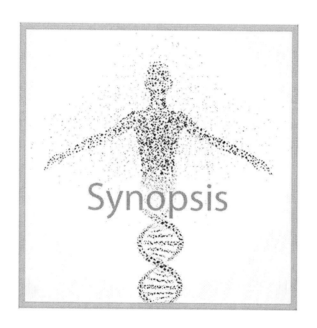

Synopsis

Explore and identify cellular imprinting from:

❖ Familial lineages passed down through DNA.

❖ Prenatal and Perinatal environment specific to mother's own experiences and stress levels.

❖ Relationship patterns modeled by parents and family system dynamics throughout childhood.

❖ Identities and roles projected onto the client during childhood through significant relationships such as parents, siblings, grandparents, coaches, teachers and spiritual advisors; and reinforced within multiple arenas of functioning such as home, school and community.

❖ Emotional, psychological, physical and sexual abuse experienced throughout childhood/adolescence.

❖ Neglect and chronic stress from growing up in chaotic, emotionally unsafe, family environments.

Explore and identify:

❖ Client's defense mechanisms that have developed in response to stress/trauma.

❖ Client's dysfunctional behavioral and relationship patterns that have developed in response to imprinting and conditioning in an unconscious attempt to get their emotional and physical needs met.

The therapist's role and responsibility:

❖ Create a safe and sacred environment to ensure that the client has the greatest opportunity to surrender to the change they desire to become and experience.

❖ Listen with their 'third ear' and reflect back to the client what it is the client communicates without even realizing it. In doing so, what the client really believes and what they truly desire begins to reveal itself.

❖ Assist the client in reorienting from an 'external locus of control' to an 'internal locus of control' in assigning responsibility for whatever the client is experiencing that is unwelcome and unwanted. This will shift client's inherent victimology and minimize their patterns of self-judgment and subsequent projections.

❖ Assist the client in increasing awareness around the environmental stimuli that triggers their respective imprints and subsequent reactivity by helping them identify and create 'space' between the stimuli, the physiological activation and subsequent emotional reactivity. By creating such a 'space', the client learns how to develop more neutral responses to the stimuli. This begins the process of dissolving the imprints because they are no longer being reinforced through the unconscious cycles of physical activation/emotional reactivity.

❖ Assist the client in developing mindfulness practices that help shift from mental preoccupation and dissociative tendencies in response to chronic stress towards a more body-centered focus and awareness. Breathwork and meditation is an integral part of creating this fundamental shift.

❖ Recognize that their capacity to assist the client in letting go of what no longer serves them will always be limited by their own ability to do the same; so it is imperative that the therapist be continuously engaged in their own process of healing *Beyond the Imprint.*

Additional Themes:

❖ Participation in **BTI** will result in the client's identity and behavioral/relationship patterns to shift.

❖ The focus of **BTI** is to assist the client in becoming 'the change' they wish to experience. The focus is not to ensure that their relationships survive this change.

❖ Despite the pain and suffering experienced by the client; they will defend their dysfunctional behavioral and relationship patterns because their personal identity has developed around these patterns.

❖ When these patterns, roles and identities are challenged by the therapist; the client's fear and subsequent resistance is experienced as an impending existential crisis. *"If I'm not this then who am I?"*

❖ Resistance is part of the process and is an unconscious attempt to ensure that current roles, identities and relationships continue. Encouraging the client to just notice it, rather than judge it, will ensure their ability to move through their fear and resistance with minimal discomfort.

❖ When the client changes; then everything that they are in relation to changes and that can be very uncomfortable and unsettling for family members and colleagues who are not participating in the therapeutic process.

❖ The focus of **BTI** is to assist the client in achieving the change they desire to become. The focus of **BTI** is never to ensure the continuation of their current, dysfunctional relationship patterns.

❖ Trauma imprinting occurs when the individual experiences something that is so overwhelming and threatening that the memory becomes 'flash-frozen' in the frequency of fear at the cellular/molecular level.

❖ This makes the individual vulnerable to cycle through similar experiences throughout the course of their lifetime because their vibratory frequency now has them in resonance with similar experiences. This pattern is always playing out at the unconscious, cellular level.

❖ Client participation in the **BTI** therapeutic process requires a tremendous amount of trust and courage as well as a willingness to surrender their defense mechanisms so that they can achieve increased visibility, transparency and vulnerability.

❖ **BTI** is a modality that does not require years of therapy; thereby ensuring that prior co-dependent relationship patterns are not reinforced within the therapeutic venue.

❖ Since trauma imprinting is cellular and physiologically-based, additional support within the nutritional and somatic framework to support the brain and body is vital for the client to access during this pivotal and critical juncture in their personal healing process.

Expressions of Trauma/Cellular Imprinting:

❖ Fear
❖ Anger
❖ Violence
❖ Control
❖ Addiction
❖ Competition
❖ Victimology
❖ Defensiveness
❖ Attachments
❖ Reactivity
❖ Manipulation
❖ Co-Dependency
❖ Mental/Emotional/Physical Imbalance

Expressions of Beyond the Imprint:

❖ Unconditional Love
❖ Gratitude
❖ Humility
❖ Surrender
❖ Cooperation
❖ Trust
❖ Detachment
❖ Moderation
❖ Equanimity
❖ Inter-Dependency
❖ Transparency
❖ Honesty
❖ Vulnerability
❖ Mental/Emotional/Physical Balance

BTI Therapy's efficacy is extremely limited for:

- ❖ Anyone who has not reached the adolescent stage of having developed meta-cognition and the critical thinking skills necessary for self-reflection.

- ❖ Individuals meeting the criteria for *Psychosis* or *Personality Disorders*.

Author's Imprint

John and Angela

John Francis Xavier O'Connell graduated from *Brooklyn Polytech* as a Civil Engineer and moved to Toronto to work for *Pitts, Johnson, Drake and Perrini* who were contracted to build the Toronto subway system. Angela Mary McGowan was working as the secretary for Mr. Pitts, Mr. Johnson, Mr. Drake and Mr. Perrini. It was 1952 and the *New York Yankees* and the *Brooklyn Dodgers* had made it to the World Series. John, having been born and raised on baseball in Brooklyn, won the office 'pool' on the '52 series, and as the story goes; Angela, in an effort to minimize her losses, walked up to John and asked him out for a beer, suggesting that he pay for the occasion with his winnings. They were engaged on their second date and married three months later. And the rest, as they say, is history.

In my mind, this was the beginning of 'us'. I have always been intrigued by the notion that had the cosmic wheel spun in such a way that the *Yankees* and *Dodgers* had not made it to the World Series that year, 'us' and 'I' would never have come into existence. It also begins to explain why I spent so much time playing baseball and drinking beer while growing up in Toronto.

Tish, Dan and Kate

John and Angela had three children: Tish, Dan and Kate. Tish and Dan were born eighteen months apart. Kate arrived four years later in 1961 and was often described by her mother as *"the best mistake your father and I ever made"*.

Tish was quiet and introverted with very few friends who was conscripted at an early age by her mother to clean house and care-take her younger siblings. She was a straight 'A' student and followed directions religiously. She rarely left the house, but rather, stayed inside reading, doing homework, drawing and completing chores. In a telephone conversation some forty years later with her younger sister, Tish would acknowledge that she had probably been depressed since childhood.

Dan was born with Celiac disease. In 1957 there were few foods that could be substituted for all of the foods that Dan was unable to eat. Consequently, at two years of age, Dan almost died. A great deal of attention had been given to Dan, given his tenuous grasp on life during his first four years. This would certainly explain his reaction to the arrival of Kate, who would shift his mother's focus away from him for the next thirty-nine years.

Kate adored her older brother and, in turn, he would initiate her into childhood through a series of 'trials by fire', usually centered on a sport. This way, when Kate came home with broken bones, cuts, scrapes, bruises, and concussions; the discussion usually centered on whether or not Kate should be playing with the older boys. The discussion never centered on how someone could get knocked unconscious during a friendly game of football.

Dan taught Kate how to catch a baseball by standing ten feet away from her and throwing it as hard as he could at her head. By the age of seven, Kate was such an accomplished baseball player that all of the priests at *St. Bonaventure's* convened a special meeting to discuss whether the rules could be changed to allow her to play in the boy's hardball league. Apparently, Kate's skills at shortstop had made such an impression, that forty years later, Father David Collins, who had grown up across the street from the O'Connell's and who was presiding over the graveside ceremony of her father, asked her if she still played. Kate couldn't help but wonder what a forty-six year old female baseball player would look like. She secretly hoped that she didn't and assuaged her fears by rationalizing that if she did; it was somehow connected to the experience of standing next to her father's coffin and it would eventually pass in time with her grief.

When Kate was five years old, she was preparing for kindergarten and mistakenly asked her brother what school was like. He told her it was a place you went every day to get the strap. At the time, Dan was having a contest with Martin Rainey to see who could get the strap the most often that year. Dan was nine years old. Seven years later, Kate made her brother extremely proud by being the first one in their family to be expelled from *St. Bonaventure's*. She was also the first person in the history of the school to be expelled without ever getting the strap.

All of the O'Connell children were extremely smart. Their father was a Professional Engineer educated by the Jesuits. He knew the answer to any question his children could possibly ask him and he would calculate these answers on a slide ruler he always carried in his shirt pocket. Their mother was a writer who was extremely well read in classic and contemporary literature. She spent most of her adult life trying to pursue her own writing career; despite being a mother and wife during the 1960's and '70's. This juggling act was a source of great frustration on her part, and great tension within the household. The O'Connell children have fuzzy memories of their mother taking her *Underwood* typewriter into the carport and locking herself in the blue *Belair* in order to get away from the chaos inside the house. This chaos usually centered on the conflictual relationship between Dan and Kate. Tish would later reveal that she left home at eighteen because she couldn't stand listening to her two younger siblings fight anymore. Kate believes that Tish left home mostly because she couldn't stand being around their mother anymore.

Angela

When Kate was three years old, Angela O'Connell was diagnosed with breast cancer. She was given a radical mastectomy and extensive radiation after which it was disclosed to her that the cancer had spread and she had six months to live. She was told to go home and make plans for her children. At the time, it was determined that John could not raise three children on his own. Plans were made for each child to go and live with a different relative. This decision makes sense when you take two things into account. It was 1964 and single fathers were uncommon. Also, when Angela's father had lost his first wife, their three daughters were sent to a convent to be raised by nuns until he remarried Angela's mother.

Angela's cancer would later reveal itself to Kate as a family secret. Despite Tish and Dan being older and having some understanding as to the significance of what was unfolding, Kate had none. In addition, during Angela's surgery, Tish and Dan were sent across the street to stay with neighbors. Kate was sent to live with Angela's best friend and John's business partner. As the story goes, when Kate returned home some three weeks later; *"she was covered from head to toe with bruises"*. The explanation was that their youngest son had inflicted those bruises on her when they had played together. It wasn't until Kate was an adult did she do the math on her fingers and realized that he would have only been 18 months old at that time and was unlikely to have been the perpetrator of such obvious abuse. Kate always wondered why her mother never did the math on her fingers; especially after her best friend, the matriarch of this family, committed suicide and it was openly discussed at her funeral that she was emotionally unstable and had physically abused her own children.

Kate's earliest memory is of pressing her face up to the living room window and desperately waiting and hoping for her brother and sister to come home from school. She would visually fixate on a colored dot off in the distance and wait for it to get bigger and bigger with the hope that it was either Tish or Dan on their way home. The memory had more to do with feelings of desperation and wanting to be rescued from the bottom of a dark hole, than the eager anticipation of playmates returning home. Kate often wondered as an adult what it must have been like to be left all day, at the age of three, with a woman who had just been told she had only six months to live. Dan mentioned to Kate once that he remembered the woman who went to the hospital in 1964 and that it was not the same woman who came home. Kate only knew the woman who had come home. It was the same woman who had written the family 'script'.

The Script

It is probably fitting that the family script was written by Angela, considering that she was the writer in the family. It was also fitting that it was written in first person since everything that happened with the O'Connell's, individually or collectively, happened for no other reason than to serve the emotional, physical and psychological needs of the author. Initially, all members of the O'Connell household made a nonverbal agreement to follow it. What makes this story interesting is to watch how every family member responded to this non-verbal contract by trying to serve the needs of one individual while maintaining some semblance of emotional autonomy and integrity.

John, primarily relied on his *Jesuit* training of selflessness, penance and suffering. He woke up every day, put his pants on one leg at a time and went to the same job for thirty-three years. He came home for lunch and dinner at the same time every day, but not before calling to see if Angela needed anything picked up at the store. He spent his weekends doing outside chores and light household repairs. He had one friend whom he got to go fishing with occasionally, until that one friend woke up one morning and had a massive heart attack while he was putting his pants on, one leg at a time. John never bothered to replace him; a possible strategy designed to minimize any future loss. John loomed large over the children as a patriarchal presence in the event that Angela was at her wit's end and couldn't handle the kids. Angela, in her inability to cope with much, was always at her wit's end. Consequently, the words *"wait 'till your father gets home!"* often rang out through the well-manicured, middle-class, suburban, ranch-style house.

Tish, who was born with the majority of 'good and reverent' genes, became almost 'saintly' in her compliance with the script. We often joke about how she doesn't iron anything now and her house always looks like a bomb just went off since she spent most of her childhood at home ironing, dusting and cleaning. We also realize that her house now looks like a bomb went off because she spent most of her childhood ironing, dusting, and cleaning. No one seemed bothered by the fact that she had no friends or never left the house except to go to school. Dan and Kate secretly resented her. They saw her compliance with the script as evidence of her being on the 'wrong side'.

Dan became the 'proverbial' son, emotionally distant and aloof who channeled his anxieties and anger by engaging in a physically and emotionally abusive relationship with his younger sister. He spent most of his childhood teaching her, in his words, *"how to be tough"*. He taught this to her by beating the 'crap' out of her on a daily basis under the guise of allowing her to participate in a neighborhood football, hockey, or baseball game. He was conceptually quite brilliant and, by the age of ten, had decided *"that he wanted to organize a religion when he grew up because there was a lot of money in that."* The Jesuit principal of *St. John Brebeuff Catholic High School* called Angela when Dan was in the 9th grade, expressing concerns that her son might be a communist since he was never seen without a copy of *"The Communist Manifesto"* stuffed in the pocket of his blue blazer. Dan took great delight in antagonizing the establishment while Kate took great delight in antagonizing Dan by engaging in hero worship with him. Dan decided to make the best of a 'pesky' situation. When Kate was ten years old, Dan dressed her up as *Che Guevera* for Halloween and gave her a political speech that she was required to memorize and recite as she made her way 'door to door' throughout the neighborhood. He rewarded her compliance by not stealing her candy or beating the 'crap' out of her that day.

Kate is not only the youngest, but possibly the most interesting of all of John and Angela's children. In addition to becoming Dan's punching bag, she also became Angela's emotional flotation device. Kate believes this part of the script was written when she was three years old and everyone else left the house to attend school and work and she was left at home alone with their 38 year-old mother and wife who was dying of cancer. This pattern was further branded into Kate's psyche when her older siblings left the nest and she remained behind as a flotation device for John and Angela's relationship. Kate survived this part of the script by 'joining' with her mother as a friend and confidante. Kate essentially became her mother's best friend and therapist. This arrangement was not without its 'perks'. It meant that when she arrived home from school in the 7th grade and announced that she had been expelled, Angela responded by asking, *"So what else is new?"* Kate remembers sitting down with her mother over a beer, having a good chuckle over the circumstances that led to her expulsion and discussing which school she should attend the following year. Kate was also experiencing the benefits of being the youngest child in a family who was being parented by two people who were really tired by the time she had reached adolescence. This arrangement, however, also came at a cost. When Kate was thirteen years old, she manifested an aggressive autoimmune disorder. Kate often wonders if she was just taking over on a deep, unconscious level where others had left off.

Drugs and Alcohol

Somehow, for reasons no one is quite sure of, including the doctors, Angela did not die in 1964. Nor did she die in '65, '66, '67, '68, or '69. And despite implied threats to the contrary, Angela hung on until 2000. This close and prolonged brush with death became a very important part of the script. After this scare and Angela's subsequent, chronic ill-health; it was understood by everyone in the family, that violating the terms contracted to in the family script could lead to the untimely demise of the matriarch and no one was willing to 'chance it'. No one in the family wanted to be responsible for killing Mom by directly addressing her psychological and emotional dysfunction, which seemed to have a stranglehold on the entire family. That was the implied threat. If you challenged the script, Mom will die. Instead, everyone chose to channel it in uniquely personal and creative ways.

With the exception of Tish, everyone drank. Not to be entirely left on the sidelines though, Tish used food the same way everyone else used alcohol. Dan and Kate, explored drugs as well. Kate, despite being the youngest, by far, exceeded everyone's expectations by combining drugs and alcohol with high-risk behaviors.

What was really interesting is that if you kept to the inferred rules of the script, you were allowed to explore alternative states of consciousness without being challenged. The rules were very simple and easy to follow. Stay in school and achieve academic excellence; don't get arrested; don't kill yourself or anyone else and don't embarrass the family. If you could follow these rules, no one was going to question why you were consistently coming home at sunrise; why the front right side of your car suddenly caved in, or why all of your ribs on the left side were broken after a sunny day of skiing at *Horseshoe Valley*.

What made it difficult to discern these behaviors as 'unhealthy', was that they were woven through rich traditions such as the Chieftain's, Waterford crystal, gourmet food, wine and whiskey, trips to Ireland and Cape Cod, Irish humor, individual achievements and lengthy, intelligent conversations at the dinner table in which everyone was expected to contribute. In other words, the O'Connell's wore their dysfunction much like the family crest that adorned their fireplace – proudly.

Rocking the Boat

After marrying and starting a family, Kate decided in the mid-'90's that she wanted to address her lengthy relationship with alcohol while in an unhealthy relationship with her husband. She began a long and exhaustive self-inventory which eventually led to her recovery from alcohol and substance abuse. It was only after coming to the startling conclusion that she was an alcoholic, was Kate able to consider the remote possibility that her parents might also be alcoholics. She was puzzled at how much easier it was to come to terms with her own issues with alcohol and how difficult it was to logically conclude the same issues were true for her parents despite all of the evidence to support this conclusion. In other words, it was as plain as the extensive collection of Waterford decanters filled with alcohol and on display in the living room window for the entire world passing by to see. And yet, it was clearly an effective and clever disguise because it had taken Kate thirty-three years to recognize the underlying pathology behind all of that sparkling alcohol. Coming to this conclusion as it related to her parents, felt like the ultimate act of betrayal. Realizing that she was in uncharted territory and on shaky ground, Kate decided not to rewrite any part of the script that did not exclusively involve her. This felt like a safe strategy, one that was sure to maintain everyone's comfort level. Well, clearly Kate was still suffering from some neurological impairment connected to LSD, magic mushrooms and *The Rolling Stones* in Rich Stadium in Buffalo on July 4th sometime during the late '70's. Whatever response she expected to get when she announced to her family of origin that she was an alcoholic and wasn't going to be drinking anymore; it was not the response she got. They looked at her as if she had just announced that she was divorcing her husband and taking their son to go live with a Cherokee medicine woman and shaman in the Adirondacks. Three years later, realizing that she had, in effect, already 'rocked the boat' and everyone was still alive and breathing; Kate decided to go for broke. She divorced her husband and co-founded a spiritual retreat center with a woman named *Soaring Hawk* up in the Adirondacks. It was at that point that Kate realized she had been 'rocking the boat' since conception, that it was a gift, something she did extremely well, and that she might as well start enjoying her gift by sharing it with the rest of the world as often as possible.

J.F.X.

John Francis Xavier was holding Angela when she 'dropped' her body on February 25, 2000. She had been diagnosed with cancer of the esophagus a year earlier. She had begun to experience episodes of dementia and during her more lucid moments they had decided not to seek treatment, given the scope of her accumulative health issues. John had kept to the agreement, never deviating from the script. Through his selfless devotion, strength of character, generosity and love for his wife; he modeled the positive attributes of the family script which Angela had authored many years before. After burying Angela on the top of a hillside in the middle of a blizzard, everyone held their breath in hopes that John would finally choose to experience life and not be in a hurry to follow his wife of forty-seven years. After all, there were all of those projects and hobbies that had accumulated over the years. He had model ships to build, an Irish harp to carve, a few trips to take, and graduations to attend. Two years later, John was diagnosed with renal failure and spent the next five years undergoing dialysis on a daily basis. In the early summer of 2007, he was rushed to the ICU with breathing difficulties. A large mass was found in his right lung and biopsied. He was given seven weeks to live. John related this news to his children and grandchildren as evidence that he was "*circling the drain a little bit faster*". John was as pragmatic as he was Irish. In response to this unwelcome news, John made the decision to unplug from dialysis and allow his body to shut down gradually over the course of several days. He marked the day he expected to 'drop his body' on a calendar.

On July 9th, 2007, Kate turned forty-six. At 8:53 p.m. she was holding her father's face between her hands when he took his last breath. Her brother Dan was in the room standing next to her. No one could have anticipated the healing that would occur between them for having shared that brief moment in time together. It was not linear, therefore it cannot be measured. It can only be noticed. Nothing short of a nuclear bomb could have impacted this family more than their father had during the last week of his life. He had turned everything upside down. He had finally rewritten the script. He had 'shown up', and in response, his children and grandchildren had been given permission to 'show up'. As a result, everyone was changed forever. Hopefully these changes will now be encoded in the cells of future generations of the O'Connell family.

Healing Beyond My Imprints

As identified earlier, one of the first significant carvings which began to change my shape was in response to the first word I spoke. And because my first word was not 'bike' or 'car' or 'ball', my shape took on the carving:

"That can't be true because she's not that special."

This initial carving deepened throughout childhood and further changed my shape to include the frequent projection:

"Your full of shit and don't know what you're talking about."

So when we add to that my imprinting from conception; which identified that my very existence was a mistake, and my conditioning from the age of three; which inferred that my primary purpose was to ensure the survival and well-being of others, a very clear picture begins to emerge regarding how I was shaped; including all of my dysfunctional behavioral and relationship patterns that became chronic expressions of that shape.

Throughout adolescence, I defended against the pain and anxiety of my unconscious limiting beliefs about myself that stemmed from my imprints by being chronically impaired and in opposition to almost everything in my environment that represented authority and external control mechanisms.

Throughout adulthood, my patterns extended to include 'rescuing' the individuals who I danced with in significant relationship. It was my unconscious belief that this is what it looked like when you loved someone. I also believed that my attempt to ensure their survival and well-being would be reciprocated in the form of their undying gratitude until *"death do us part"*. Much to my surprise, my distorted expressions of love always ended up being reciprocated with their undying resentment and their need to control me, which caused these relationships to eventually dissolve from the toxicity of extreme co-dependency.

In response to taking on the deep and limiting belief that *"I was full of shit and didn't know what I was talking about"*; my patterns also included the tendency to abdicate the self by putting individuals I admired on a pedestal. This allowed me to become the perpetual student always seeking out knowledge from those I deemed to be *'wisdom-keepers'*. After all, I could never allow myself to connect to the possibility that I might actually know something because going against the grain of my unconscious imprinting was far too dangerous and anxiety-provoking.

This never stopped me, however, from overextending myself beyond anything that could have been perceived as healthy or balanced in an effort to prove myself to others. It took me a very long time to realize that I was really just trying to prove myself to myself.

And one day, at the age of twelve, while I was trying to prove myself to myself, I experienced a remarkable event in response to a significant trauma that caused me to leave my body in such a way that I found myself on 'the other side' negotiating the terms of coming back. I experienced the memory of this event as a dawning awareness that would gradually reveal itself to me over the next forty years and inform the manner in which my life would unfold.

This event also provided me with my first reference to non-duality beyond the physical, the ego and the personality. What was most striking was my profound awareness of being held in a space of non-judgment, complete acceptance and pure unconditional love. I understood that it didn't matter which choice I made. And as it turned out, I did choose to come back when I was shown that I would create something significant that would help a lot of people. The negotiation had to do with my need to be reassured that I would never again experience such trauma if I chose to return.

I now believe that I came back to create this modality and that this book is the vehicle for sharing it with others. It includes all of the hallmarks that I recognized and followed along the way that allowed me to arrive at this very place. It includes all of my guidance going back to my near-death experience at the age of twelve that has allowed me to be here now. It is extremely profound because this creation has become the proof to me that I am here, that I am aware, and that I do know what I am talking about.

I now know that I came back to have these experiences and to create the vehicle that would allow me to heal from these experiences. I came back for all of it because none of it could have happened without the other. What's ironic is that 'the hook' that inspired me to come back during this negotiation was the identification that what I came back to do would be for the benefit of others. Given my imprinting and subsequent patterns, it's entirely possible that I may not have come back had I understood that it was for my own benefit.

So it turns out that what I have done is something of a milestone in my own development. I have created this modality under the auspices of helping others, but what I have really done is to help myself reach a whole new level of acceptance, appreciation and awareness.

And because all of my experiences have led to each development unfolding in a manner that was necessary and caused this to occur; my current expression of being of service to others is now imbued with much more love, honesty, humility and gratitude.

How elegant life is that the very 'script' that is required as a vehicle for healing and transformation is created and finds expression from our deepest wounds.

"The wound is the place

where the light enters you."

- Rumi -

Appendix A

The following is a summary from **CCHR** listing a handful of individuals who were under Senate Finance Committee investigation for the roles they played in furthering sales for Big Pharma in exchange for large monetary donations:

Nada Stotland: The 2008 APA President, Stotland serves on the Board of the National Mental Health Association (now called Mental Health America), a group that received over $3 million in pharmaceutical company funding in one year alone. In 2008, Pfizer donated at least $500,000 to Mental Health America while Eli Lilly donated $600,000. Stotland is on the speakers' bureau for Pfizer and GlaxoSmithKline (GSK).

David Kupfer: A member of the DSM-IV Task Force and Chair of the DSM-V Task Force. He has been a consultant to Eli Lilly & Co., Johnson and Johnson, Solvay/Wyeth, Servier and also sat on the advisory boards of Forest Labs and Pfizer. In 2008, Kupfer also disclosed that he had been a consultant for Forest Pharmaceuticals, Pfizer Inc., Hoffman La Roche, Lundbeck and Novartis.

Dilip V. Jeste: APA Trustee and Member of the DSM-V Task Force is a consultant to Bristol-Myers Squibb, Lilly, Janssen, Solvay/Wyeth and Otsuka; honoraria from Bristol-Myers Squibb, Janssen and Otsuka; received "supplemental support to NIMH-funded grants" from Astra Zeneca, Bristol-Myers Squibb, Eli Lilly, and Janssen in the form of donated medication for the study,

"Metabolic Effects of Newer Antipsychotics in Older Patients." Jeste's 2008 APA disclosure for the DSM-V Task Force stated he received honorarium from Abbott, AstraZeneca, Bristol-Myers Squibb, Eli Lilly Janssen, Pfizer-Eisai, Solvay-Wyeth and Otsuka. He also received consulting fees from nine pharmaceutical companies.

Steven Sharfstein: *Former APA president who sat on the Board of Directors of the American Psychiatric Foundation (APF), an organization formed by the APA that lists 17 major pharmaceutical companies as its corporate adviser. Since 1992, he has been President and CEO of Sheppard Pratt Health System and in 2002, he signed on 6 pharmaceutical companies to test their products at Sheppard Pratt. He signed contracts with Eli Lilly & Co., Merck and Janssen Research Foundation.*

Joseph Biederman: *Chief of the Program in Pediatric Psychopharmacology, Massachusetts General Hospital, Biederman has received research funds from 15 pharmaceutical companies. The New York Times exposed how Joseph Biederman earned $1.6 million in consulting fees from drug makers between 2000 and 2007 but did not report all of this income to Harvard University officials. His marketing of the theory that children have "bipolar" was attributed to the increase in antipsychotic drug sales for pediatric use in the United States—today 2.5 million children. Following exposure of his conflicts, he stepped down from a number of industry-funded clinical trials. In March 2009, in newly released court documents, Biederman was reported to have promised drug maker Johnson & Johnson in advance that his studies on the antipsychotic drug Risperidone would prove the drug to be effective when used on preschool age children.*

Melissa DelBello: *Research psychiatrist, University of Cincinnati was cited for her failure to disclose to the university much of what she had earned from pharmaceutical companies. In 2002, she was the lead author of a study that reported some patients* benefited from the antipsychotic drug Seroquel, which is manufactured by AstraZeneca, which paid her $100,000 in 2003 and $80,000 in 2004. DelBello disclosed that she'd received $100,000 from the company between 2005 and 2007, but federal investigators discovered it was more than double that— $238,000.

Frederick Goodwin: Former National Institute of Mental Health (NIMH) director, Goodwin earned at least $1.3 million between 2000 and 2007 for giving marketing lectures to physicians on behalf of drug makers—a fact he did not reveal to the audience, broadcaster or producers of "The Infinite Mind," that he hosted on the National Public Radio during its 10-year run.

Charles Nemeroff: Professor and Chairman of Psychiatry and Behavioral Sciences, Emory University School of Medicine in Atlanta. From 2000 through 2006, Nemeroff received just over $960,000 from GlaxoSmithKline (GSK), but only disclosed no more than $35,000 to Emory. Between 2000 and 2007, Charles Nemeroff earned more than $2.8 million from various drug makers but failed to report at least $1.2 million. He signed a letter in 2004 promising Emory administrators that he would earn less than $10,000 a year from GSK but on the same day he was at a hotel earning $3,000 of what would become $170,000 in income from the company—17 times greater than the figure he agreed upon. He was the principal investigator for a five-year $3.9 billion grant financed by the NIMH for which GSK provided the drugs, during which he received more than the annual $10,000 threshold allowed from the company. In 2003, he coauthored a favorable review of three therapies in Nature Neuroscience failing to mention his significant financial interests in these, including owning the patent for one of the treatments— a lithium patch. Nemeroff has consulted for 21 drug and device companies simultaneously. In 1991 Nemeroff testified before the FDA on behalf of Eli Lilly in hearings into Prozac, saying that the drug did not cause suicidal acts of ideation—yet 13 years later, the FDA concluded the opposite and issued a black box warning about suicide risks.

Martin Keller: *Professor of Psychiatry and Human Behavior at Brown University, chairman of the psychiatry department at the Alpert Medical School, Keller's study (329) on GSK's Paxil use in children and adolescents and its authors have been fiercely criticized in medical journals for allegedly misrepresenting data, suppressing information linking the drug to suicidal tendencies and reaching a conclusion unsupported by the relevant data. There are also claims that a GSK-affiliated employee ghostwrote Study 329, while Keller et al. made huge sums of money from the antidepressant manufacturer. In 1999, it was disclosed that while serving as chief of the psychiatry department at Brown University, Keller earned more than $842,000 from Pfizer, Bristol-Myers Squibb, Wyeth-Ayerst and Eli Lilly, makers of antidepressants he "lauded in a series of medical research reports." After a three-year criminal investigation by the Attorney General's Office, Brown University "agreed to return $300,170" of taxpayer money to the state of Massachusetts for psychiatric research Keller's psychiatry department never performed. Additionally, Keller did not disclose the extent of his financial ties with companies to the medical journals that published his research—this included $93,199 in 1998. In the same year that Keller authored a review article in Biological Psychiatry, and concluded that the newer antidepressants were more effective, he received $77,400 in personal income and $1.2 million in research funding from the makers of two of these drugs.*

Alan Schatzberg *was appointed APA President in May 2009, despite the exposure of his conflict of interest. As exposed in The New York Times and other media, Schatzberg owned $6 million equity in drug developer Corcept Therapeutics at the same time that he was principle investigator in an NIH-funded, Stanford-based study of Corcept's drug mifepristone. Schatzberg had* initiated the patent application on mifepristone to "treat psychotic depression" in 1997. He co-founded Corcept in 1998, and in 1999, extended the NIH grant for the study of psychotic depression to include mifepristone.

Thomas Spencer: Assistant Director of the Pediatric Psychopharmacology Unit at Massachusetts General Hospital and Associate Professor of Psychiatry, Harvard Medical School, he is under Senate investigation for reportedly failing to disclose at least $1 million in earnings from drug companies between 2000 and 2007.

Karen Wagner: Professor, University of Texas Medical Branch at Galveston reportedly failed to disclose more than $150,000 in payments from GSK. Between 2000 and 2008, Wagner had worked on NIH-funded studies on the use of Paxil to treat teenage depression and was a co-researcher on Study 329 (See Keller). In 2001, when study 329 was published, the company reportedly paid her $18,255. Between 1998 and 2001, she was one of several researchers participating in more than a dozen industry-funded pediatric trials of antidepressants and other drugs. In her Zoloft study, Wagner said she had received "research support" from several drug makers, including Pfizer, but did not disclose she had received "sizeable payments" from Pfizer for work related to the study. Between 2000 and 2005 GSK paid her $160,404, but only $600 was disclosed to the university. In 2002, Eli Lily also paid her over $11,000, which was not disclosed.

Timothy Wilens: Associate Professor of Psychiatry at Harvard Medical School in Boston allegedly failed to report that between 2000 and 2007 he had earned at least $1.6 million from drug makers. Federal grants received Dr. Joseph Biederman (above) and Wilens were administered by Massachusetts General Hospital, which in 2005 won $287 million in such grants. He is under Congressional investigation.

CCHR further reported that:

The Senate Finance Committee also requested the financial records of **NAMI**, *a group long accused of being a covert marketing arm of the pharmaceutical industry. The mental health alliance, which is hugely influential in many state capitols, has refused for years to disclose specifics of its fund-raising, saying the details were private. But according to documents obtained by The New York Times, drug makers from 2006 to 2008 contributed nearly $23 million to the alliance, about three-quarters of its donations."*

While the **National Alliance on Mental Illness (NAMI)**, *claims to be an advocacy organization for people with "mental illness," its actions indicate otherwise. The group opposed the black box warnings on antidepressants causing suicide for under 18 year olds in 2004, and black box warnings on ADHD drugs causing heart attack, stroke and sudden death in children in 2006, when you look at their biggest source of funding: Pharma.*

"In the end these three things matter most:

How well did you live?

How deeply did you love?

How fully did you let go? "

- Buddha -

Made in the USA
Middletown, DE
28 June 2017